Barrie Keeffe
Plays: 1

Gimme Shelter
(Gem, Gotcha, Getaway)

Barbarians
(Killing Time, Abide With Me, In the City)

Gimme Shelter: 'One of the most important and exciting social documents seen for a very long time . . . Barrie Keeffe speaks with a voice of absolute authority. He shows us the human detritus of the Welfare State, and his rejects are all the more affecting for being young and energetic and in theory the recipients of egalitarian education . . . To his great credit, the author does not make any glib political points and offers no easy solutions.' *Sunday Telegraph*
'Keeffe plays idea against idea, emotion against emotion, in the text that is practically a musical score.' *New York Post*

Barbarians: Barrie Keeffe has a remarkable insight into the characters of these young people . . . He puts it all into skilful and often highly comic dialogue that bears the same relation to everyday Cockney as O'Casey's speech does to everyday Dublin.' *Financial Times*
'I cannot recommend the plays too highly simply because Keeffe tackles the problems of today with gusto, compassion, energy and detailed knowledge of the victims. He is the only playwright in this country concerned with the reality and not the fantasy of this country's youth.' *Time Out*

Barrie Keeffe was born in East London in 1945. He was an actor with the National Youth Theatre and a journalist before turning to writing. His plays have been performed in 20 countries and include *A Mad World, My Masters* (Joint Stock, 1977), *Frozen Assets* (RSC, 1978), *Sus* (Soho Poly and Royal Court, 1979), *Bastard Angel* (RSC, 1980) and *Wild Justice* (Theatre Royal, Stratford East, 1991). He was resident writer for the Shaw Theatre (1977) and for the RSC (1978). He won the Paris Critics Prix Révélation in 1978 for *Gotcha*, the Giles Cooper Best Radio Play Award in 1978 for *Heaven Scent* and the Edgar Allan Poe Award in 1982 for his screenplay *The Long Good Friday*. He has directed some of his work in London and Amsterdam and was an ambassador for the United Nations in their 50th anniversary year (1995).

BARRIE KEEFFE

Plays: 1

Gimme Shelter
Gem
Gotcha
Getaway

Barbarians
Killing Time
Abide With Me
In the City

Introduced by the author

Methuen Drama

METHUEN CONTEMPORARY DRAMATISTS

1 3 5 7 9 10 8 6 4 2

This collection first published in the United Kingdom in 2001 by
Methuen Publishing Limited
215 Vauxhall Bridge Road, London SW1V 1EJ

Gimme Shelter first published by Eyre Methuen in 1977
Copyright © 1977 by Barrie Keeffe

Barbarians first published by Eyre Methuen in 1978
Copyright © 1978 by Barrie Keeffe

This collection and introduction copyright © 2001 by Barrie Keeffe

The right of the author to be identified as the author of these works
has been asserted by him in accordance with the
Copyright, Designs and Patents Act, 1988

Methuen Publishing Limited Reg. No. 3543167

A CIP catalogue record for this book
is available from the British Library

ISBN 0 413 76450 8

Typeset by MATS, Southend-on-Sea, Essex
Printed and bound in Great Britain by
Cox & Wyman Ltd, Reading, Berkshire

Contents

In loving memory
of
Verity Bargate

Chronology
of first performances

The Substitute (Granada TV)	1972
Only a Game (Shaw Theatre; BBC Radio)	1973;1978
A Certain Vincent (trans. with Jules Croiset; Amsterdam, then Shaw Theatre)	1974
Good Old Uncle Jack (BBC Radio)	1974
Anything Known? (BBC Radio)	1974
Pigeon Skyline (BBC Radio)	1974
A Sight of Glory (National Youth Theatre at Cockpit Theatre)	1975
Scribes (University Theatre, Newcastle, then Greenwich Theatre)	1975
Gem (Soho Poly, then Thames TV)	1975
Heaven Scent (BBC Radio)	1975
Here Comes the Sun (National Youth Theatre at Jeanetta Cochrane)	1976
Gotcha (Soho Poly, then BBC TV)	1976
Abide With Me (Soho Poly, then Granada TV)	1976
Gimme Shelter (Soho Poly, then Royal Court)	1977
Up the Truncheon (National Youth Theatre at Shaw Theatre)	1977
Killing Time (National Youth Theatre at Soho Poly)	1977
A Mad World, My Masters (Joint Stock at Young Vic, then the Roundhouse)	1977
Nipper (BBC TV)	1977
Barbarians (Greenwich Theatre)	1977
Frozen Assets (RSC at the Warehouse, then BBC Radio)	1978
Hanging Around (BBC TV)	1978
Waterloo Sunset (BBC TV)	1978
She's So Modern (Queen's Theatre, Hornchurch)	1978
Sus (Soho Poly, then Royal Court)	1979
Bastard Angel (RSC at the Warehouse)	1980
The Long Good Friday (Calendar Films)	1981

Introduction

Daniel Farson's photograph 'Boy and Dog' on the cover
of this book was on the wall above my desk all the time I
was writing these plays. I bought it from a stall in
Greenwich Market when I started thinking about the
plays. The boy in the photograph was just how I imagined
the Kid in *Gotcha* and Jan in *Barbarians* would have been as
kids: a haunting mixture of defiance and vulnerability; a
determination not to be beaten down. I also liked the
protective stance and stare of his dog. If only the Kid had
had a guarding dog.

I always play music when writing to get me, and keep
me, in the mood of the scenes. A cheer normally goes up
from my neighbours when they stop hearing the same
tunes day after day. I've indicated the songs I played in
these texts and they've usually been played in productions
I've been involved in. I wish I'd stuck to my guns for a
production of *Barbarians* in Wiesbaden; Kraut punk – need
I say more?

These two trilogies I think of as my youth plays (or
should that be 'yuff'?). I was anxious to get them down
before I forgot what it was like to be young.

The six plays are dedicated in loving memory to Verity
Bargate, the co-founder with Fred Proud and from 1975
the artistic director of the Soho Poly Theatre in Riding
House Street, W1 – closest I've got to the West End with
my work.

I'd had one theatre play produced: a shambolic,
muddled and embarrassingly disastrous effort called *Only a
Game*. 'If only it were a game, anything but this rag-bag of
worn out clichés,' wrote the late Jack Tinker in the *Daily
Mail*. It's funny how I can always remember the lousy
quotes and not so the good ones. He was right as it
happens and I was encouraged reading a David Hare
interview in *Plays and Players* in which he said, given there
are so many fringe theatres sprouting all over the place, it

wasn't terribly difficult for an aspiring playwright to get his work put on.

I was recording a play for radio at Broadcasting House and was taken by the producer to the Poly, just round the corner. It was a lunchtime theatre – one-act plays of less than one hour. For me everything about it made it love at first sight. It was a scorching summer and the low-ceilinged sweaty cellar reminded me at once of the atmosphere of the Flamingo Club where I used to go for Georgie Fame and the Blue Flames in the sixties. I'd always wished a theatre experience could have the same buzz as a music gig and the Poly fitted the bill exactly. Just thirty-five hard, red wooden chairs but standing room for another seventy when occasion demanded (illegal): it was tight and almost claustrophobic – the standing audience squeezed together like rush-hour passengers on the Northern tube line. You couldn't escape and felt the actors couldn't possibly be lying because you were so close to them. The play was Howard Brenton's *The Saliva Milkshake* and I was hooked.

It was verily an arts-factory. New artists submitted their paintings for an exhibition each season and there was a new production every fortnight; one year, more than twenty new plays by mostly new writers. Pam Gems, Caryl Churchill and later Hanif Kureishi and Tony Marchant cut their teeth there. It was also a highly popular hunting-ground for TV producers, no doubt because the length of a Poly play was the same 55-minutes' duration as a TV drama slot in the days TV did one-off plays. In 1976, six Poly plays were taken up and televised.

There was another reason it became my regular fringe stamping ground: the astonishingly beautiful, witty and wise Verity. My gauche and naive East End background meant that I'd never before met anyone quite like her. She always gave you a very direct look with her stunning emerald-green eyes and could be quite sharp when irritated in her tiny cubby-hole of an office. But she'd always defuse what might have caused offence with an enormous smile and a hug: 'I meant that with enormous affection,' she'd say, irrefutably.

She seemed to know everyone in theatre, TV and film I'd only read about. After another show that sweltering summer she invited me for post-show drinks with everyone at a nearby pub in a narrow alleyway. I felt hopelessly out of depth and gauche with Verity's mates Jean Shrimpton and Terence Stamp – totally tongue-tied. Verity put me at my ease as she somehow put everyone at their ease and we spent a couple of hours sitting on the alleyway floor in the sunshine talking. 'Got anything for me?' she asked with an ambiguous grin after I'd made her laugh with my tales of woe about my *Only a Game* calamity. By chance (or was it?) I had a one-act play in my bag. I'd decided to start again as a playwright and wanted to get the simple things right, so I'd written a play about four people I knew, one day in their lives. This was *Gem*. That evening she phoned me and said she was going to put it on at the Poly. She also said 'I believe in you as a writer.'

I always reckoned, from what I'd read of the inspiration of the Royal Court and George Devine and their loyalty to their writers, and I now assuredly know, that a writer does his best work when he has total commitment to one theatre and that theatre is similarly committed to him. The Soho Poly became my home from home as did later the NYT and more recently, for at least a decade, the Theatre Royal, Stratford East with Philip Hedley.

I learned a lot from *Gem*'s director Keith Washington and the play was 'warmly received'. At the theatre there was a staff of two besides Verity and I admit I was taken aback when, because everyone had to muck in, my job at the first performance was to work the box office – a card-table by the door as you walked down the steps from the street. It was a peculiar sensation handing tickets to critics about to review your work. I had to half carry the *Sunday Times* critic Sir Harold Hobson, who had a bad leg, down the steps into the cellar. Verity used to bring in sandwiches she'd made at home for the lunchtime audience; during a season of Hungarian plays she brought in casseroles of homemade goulash each day.

When John Osborne once slagged off fringe theatre in a vitriolic August summer-silly-season essay as 'wanking in cellars', Verity was outraged, though laughed heartily when she realised hers was London's only theatre in a cellar. What she wrote on her postcard to Osborne is unprintable here.

Barry Hanson bought *Gem* for Thames Television where he was producing a season of new one-off plays, and thus began a friendship and working relationship leading up to *The Long Good Friday*. *Gem* was retitled *Not Quite Cricket* for TV. The fee enabled me to give up my job as a journalist and concentrate on writing.

'So what are you going to give me next?' asked Verity – more demanded than enquired – with the becoming-familiar half flirty, mysterious grin. I had scribbled down six or seven pages and she took them home. It was a couple of days before she phoned and invited me over for supper at her house to talk through the idea. She said the title *Gotcha* grabbed her: 'One-word titles are cheap in the *Guardian* listings advertisements,' she explained. This was the same reason a later play for her I'd called *A Rare Complication* became *Sus*.

However first of all I wrote a play for the late Michael Croft and his National Youth Theatre. He'd been my mentor when I was writing my novel *Gadabout* and had urged me to write plays. I'd been an NYT actor while at school where I learned dishearteningly but utterly that I didn't have what it took to be an actor – and anyway, I wanted to be the East London James Dean but no one was writing those kind of things. Maybe the Kid in *Gotcha* was the kind of role I'd wanted in my acting days.

A Sight of Glory, a year in the life of an East End boys' boxing club, completed, I set to work on *Gotcha* at some speed – this necessitated when Verity sent me a proof of the poster for the as-yet-unwritten play and the gob-smacking news that Keith would start rehearsing in three

weeks. She was a cunning bully of genius and real
manipulative inspiration.

She also showed me some scenes for a play she had
begun to write. Unsure how she would react and not at all
confident I was correct, I told her I thought it would work
better as a novel. She was a voracious reader of new fiction
and her house was cluttered with books. Curiously,
because she was always so broke, she only had one record
album. Since I was getting free vinyl as a part-time
reviewer I had a good excuse to start visiting her frequently
at her house in Greenwich – to give her albums. She
showed me how she was progressing with *Baby Blue*, as the
novel was then called, and I showed her how I was getting
on with *Gotcha*. *Baby Blue* came from the Bob Dylan album
she was always playing; I reckoned that, like me, she was
addicted to repetitive record playing while writing. I also
started to fancy Verity more and more. We became lovers
after the first night of *Gotcha*. She'd ordered the national
newspapers, and to wake up to the smashing reviews and
with Verity was like being in a movie of someone else's life.
The novel became *No Mama No* and was published to huge
acclaim in Britain, then in the USA and most of Europe.

We were like artful collaborators; we seemed to inspire
each other in a way I never have and am never likely to
experience again. Her novel became a much fanfared TV
production, as did *Gotcha*. And here's where I started
feeling like the boy in Farson's photograph – a boy in
trouble.

In a blaze of publicity Mrs Mary Whitehouse (boss of
the National Viewers and Listeners Association)
condemned the transmission of the play as 'one long
obscene gesture'. The punk revolution was in full flight and
the 'notorious' publicity had the effect of increasing the
play's status both in Britain and overseas. My favourite
memory of the foreign productions was the Russian
translator telling me that the play would be liked in
Moscow because it showed the 'immorality of capitalism in
decline – a scenario that could not happen in the Soviet

Union'. I idly asked about the actor playing the Kid. 'Oh, he identifies with the part totally,' came the reply. How come, if this scenario could not happen in the Soviet Union? I asked. 'Oh, he has mental problems,' said the translator with a patronising grin. Natch.

Verity's young sons Sam and Thomas (three and one-and-a-half when I first met the chaps) delighted in bringing in the increasingly hysterical newspapers when they were delivered. 'Gotcha' was a frequent headline – I found it sickening when it was used as a front-page splash for the sinking of the *Belgrano* in the *Sun*.

It was fun but slightly unreal that a play written for a 35-seater cellar was making so much news. Come August the following year, the publicity became madness. The BBC decided to repeat *Gotcha*. Verity was away attending her grandmother's funeral when the news broke. I remember Tom asking her what happens when you die. Verity said her grandmother had gone to heaven. When a few days later Elvis Presley died, Tom asked if he'd gone to heaven too. Verity said yes. 'I wonder how he's getting on with Gran?' pondered Tom.

The death of Elvis kept the news of the repeat out of sight in the press until Mrs Whitehouse discovered it listed in the *Radio Times*. She let rip with condemnations of it for containing an 'explicit sexual assault on a woman teacher' and 'the brutal sadistic kicking of the boy's genitals by a male teacher'. Not to mention some of the language. The BBC abruptly cancelled the transmission with the statement: 'It was decided by the Director-General, Ian Trethowan, that the language in *Gotcha* would not be acceptable even at a late hour.' It transpired that Mrs Whitehouse had written to the Home Secretary urging him to bring pressure on the BBC governors to have the repeat cancelled. She also claimed that after her protests about the original broadcast the then Director-General Sir Charles Curran had agreed with her criticisms and more or less apologised for the error of judgement. In a flood of letters of protest at the ban in the *Guardian* – the saga ran-

and-ran for weeks, and not only in the *Guardian* – was one
from Sir Charles in which he set out his letter to Mrs
Whitehouse. Not quite as she described it.

It earned me the tabloid-press nickname 'Controversial
Cockney Playwright' – something that took me years to
lose – and Verity and I, in cavalier mood, fanned the
flames of the controversy by, we thought, quite decently
inviting anyone who felt they were mature enough to view
Gotcha without being corrupted to see screenings of a video
of the BBC production at the Soho Poly. Our *Guardian*
invitation brought us more than 2,000 letters asking for
tickets but legal/copyright reasons meant that we had to
abandon the wake showings.

What I had conceived as a serious contribution to what
the press were calling 'The Great Education Debate' on
comprehensive schools – politicians, educationalists,
teachers all had their say; I wanted to give a voice to the
unheard kids of the system – *Gotcha* instead became a tool
in the raging debate over television censorship. Curiously,
ten years later, the BBC did transmit *Gotcha* again – in a
radio production for their schools service.

Before the banning, Verity and I decided to let the
central characters of *Gem* and *Gotcha* come face to face in a
third play to complete the *Gimme Shelter* trilogy. I was going
to call it *Let It Bleed*, hence the line in the play some
directors have such difficulty with. (Solution? The Kid cuts
his finger opening a beer can.) The trilogy went on as a
rare evening production at the Poly and, such was the
response and packed houses, it moved on to the main
house at the Royal Court. I remember meeting Verity for
tea at Fortnum and Mason's before the show. She was
wearing a huge beret, one front side pulled down to cover
her left eye. She'd made a dash from working the Poly box
office for the lunchtime show and had only time enough to
put make-up on her right eye.

Verity was already into her second novel, *Children
Crossing*, which would later receive even more extravagant
reviews than *No Mama No* here and abroad and became

another TV film. The pace of life was frenetic; looking
through my diaries of the period I wonder how we had the
energy. Perhaps we both had some subconscious feeling
that time was running out. I'd never been to so many
parties and first nights as with Verity. She was always the
last one to leave a party. As the reputation of the Poly
soared, so did the number of new plays she received,
mostly by new writers. I still can't figure out how she
managed to read them all – but she somehow did. The
then *Times* critic Irving Wardle wrote that Verity seemed
to have a water-diviner's touch for discovering first-rate
first plays. The cupboard under her stairs at home was
stacked with them and yet she somehow kept picking
winners. And writing her novels and screenplays. And
being an enviably perfect single mum actively involved
with the school's PTA.

While Verity did her million things I was reluctantly
conned by Michael Croft into writing two plays for his
NYT's twenty-fifth anniversary season. I dutifully wrote a
rock-music farce for a cast of seventy with the
appropriately dreadful title of *Up the Truncheon*, while
protesting that I really wanted to write a short three-
hander using the same characters as I'd just used in *Abide
With Me* (at the Poly, of course). I was checkmated by Croft
who triumphantly told me he'd put on both. 'You're a very
lucky fellah,' he bellowed. 'You should be grateful.
Shakespeare is the only other writer to have had two plays
performed in one NYT season – you're honoured. He's
dead.'

So began *Killing Time* with Jan, Paul and Louis a year
before their Cup-Final exploits in *Abide With Me*. This was
bought by Granada TV and I 'got into trouble again'.
When *Champions*, as it was retitled, was transmitted, Louis
Edwards, chairman of Manchester United, blew a fuse
very publicly. It became the *Daily Mirror*'s front-page lead:
'FOUL! The soccer scenes that scared off ITV.' On the
same front page was a photo of Sex Pistol Johnny Rotten
accompanying some story about his sore-throat infection.

On the bus going to get her perm for Christmas my mum
saw my story and the photo of Johnny Rotten making a V-
sign, thought it was me and got off the bus. Every Yuletide
she complained it was my fault she never had her hair
done for Christmas 1978.

During this hectic year and with for me money rolling in
for the first time, we had a first family holiday in Greece. It
was as though we never stopped talking: Verity with all her
ideas of novels to write, me sketching out ideas for *The Long
Good Friday* and hatching a plot to complete the trilogy
which became *Barbarians*. We also got in a lot of trips to
first nights of my plays in Europe. Things that began as
'wanking in a basement' have now been produced in
twenty countries, including Russia, Japan, Israel and India,
as well as Europe and the US. When overseas directors
came to London to discuss their productions I would meet
them at the Poly. They were usually shocked at how tiny
the place was, just as I was shocked when I first saw the
vastness of the German Schauspielhauses and wondered
how the trilogies could fill such spaces. One of the best first
nights in Europe came in Paris when the actors playing the
Kid in Amsterdam, Germany and Sweden came to meet
the French Kid. I was surprised, but of course very
pleased, that what I had written as very local East End
plays got the same reaction outside Britain as they did
here. I am similarly surprised that twenty-four years on
they are still regularly performed, that unfortunately they
still seem to have a pertinence. I thought they were, as one
critic described them, 'instant political theatre'.

It was a few days after we returned from Greece – me to
write *Frozen Assets* for the RSC and Verity the screenplay
for *Children Crossing* – that she discovered a lump on her left
breast. The GP diagnosed it as a possible cancerous
growth and she went into hospital the next day. She
bought a nightdress for the first time since I'd met her. The
exploratory operation showed that it was indeed cancer
and the breast was removed. I can still see her slowly
waking from the anaesthetic and instinctively feeling her

left breast. 'Thank God they haven't had to remove it,' she said drowsily. What she could feel was the protrusion of the padding covering the scar of the operation.

Verity had been a nurse in her youth. Her mother had died of cancer at the age of forty. Of course, her moods swung from despair, knowing the possibility of the worst, to optimistic defiance and joyous hope. I saw a parallel with my hero Muhammad Ali – getting pounded in a corner and yet, when all seemed lost, bouncing out against all the odds for a triumphant victory. But the cancer spread slowly to her bones. Her periods in hospital and her remissions interchanged: she lost her hair through the chemotherapy but hated wearing a wig; indeed she was the original Sinead O'Connor for style. She began to write her third novel *Tit for Tat* with a fury, and I wrote *Sus*, which was used for an outdoor Rock Against Racism show in a huge field one summer evening. Verity said, 'You always wanted to be a rock'n'roller,' as the Poly production held the attention of thousands between the bands. 'You always said you wrote plays for people who wouldn't be seen dead in a theatre. Well, here they are.' The Poly production transferred to the Royal Court. Verity was back in hospital for the first night in Sloane Square but her humour never deserted her. She sent the actors a telegram: 'If I can bribe a couple of porters to nick a stretcher for me and carry me in I'll be there cheering you on.'

As Verity's condition worsened and the cancer continued to spread she gave up her work at the Poly and raced to finish *Tit for Tat*. She insisted I keep writing and promised me that Philip Hedley, artistic director of the Theatre Royal Stratford East, believed in me as a writer as much as she did. Unlikely but true, since the musical I struggled to write, *Chorus Girls*, with Ray Davies, became a target for scorn and derision. It opened the same day as *Tit for Tat* was published.

To ensure I became legal guardian of Sam and Thomas we rushed forward our marriage: Saturday 14th February 1981, Valentine's Day, was fully booked. The registrar was astonished that I booked unlucky Friday 13th – in thirty years he'd never married anyone on that day. Verity came out of hospital the morning of the wedding, the party was crowded and bitter-sweet, and she returned to hospital early in the evening. Ray was best man. There was a lot of weeping in the house when I returned from Verity's bedside at midnight.

Verity stayed alive long enough to enjoy the superb reviews *Tit for Tat* received. She died at 1.15 p.m. on Monday 18th May. She was thirty-nine. It was strange having the post-funeral wake in the same place that three months earlier we'd had a wedding party.

As this book is published I'll be aware that her birthday this year would have been her sixtieth. But, of course, she'll always be that beautiful, blonde, green-eyed girl with the huge grin who looked and behaved far younger than anyone the age of thirty-nine had the right to.

A Chinese poem fits the bill for my last sentence:

After the fireworks,
Look,
A falling star.

Barrie Keeffe
Greenwich, 2001

Gimme Shelter

Gem
Gotcha
Getaway

Gimme Shelter was first produced as a trilogy at the Soho Poly Theatre Club, London, on 1 February 1977, with the following cast:

Kev	Phillip Joseph
Gary	Ian Sharp
Janet	Sharman MacDonald
Bill	Roger Leach
Ton	Roger Leach
Lynne	Sharman MacDonald
Kid	Philip Davis
Head	Peter Hughes

Directed by Keith Washington
Designed by Mary Moore
Lighting by Nick Chelton

The production subsequently toured Britain with Theatre Network Ltd and played a season at the Royal Court Theatre, London; the company was unchanged.

Gem

A play in three scenes

Gem was first produced on 7 July 1975 at the Soho Poly Theatre Club, London, with the following cast:

Kev	Will Knightley
Gary	Adrian Shergold
Janet	Sharman MacDonald
Bill	Michael Brodie

Directed by Keith Washington
Designed by Jane Ripley

The setting throughout is the boundary of a cricket pitch.

Music

Before and after Scene One: Suzi Quatro's 'Wild One'
Before Scene Three: Showaddywaddy's 'Three Steps to Heaven'
After Scene Three: Gary Glitter's 'Alright with the Boys'

Scene One

Morning. During the scene the light becomes brighter.

August bank holiday Monday. A bare stage, green. Stage right, part of a white cricket boundary screen. The audience is the cricket pitch.

Blackout. We hear Suzi Quatro's 'Wild One'. Lights up to reveal Kev, holding a transistor to his ear. He stares at the audience, switches off the radio.

Pause.

Kev   Oh for the summer sun and the lush green fields of England. The gentle click of leather against willow. Cucumber sandwiches for tea and swallows in the twilight. (*He shouts.*) Come on you bastards, this'll do.

Kev *sets down a plastic carrier-bag, takes out a can of beer, opens it, sips. He bounces a plastic football on his foot.*

Gary (*off*)   Here, shot, shot –

Kev *passes the ball to* **Gary** *who races onstage and kicks the ball behind the screen.*

Gary   Goal, what a goal! When's the season start? Here I am, charged up and raring to go like a bloody racehorse in his box.

Kev   This'll do, won't it?

Gary   Yeah, fine fine. Can't get further away from the pavilion than this, eh. Oi, Jan – come on.

Enter **Janet** *and* **Bill**. *She is holding one shoe.*

Janet   I thought we was supposed to be watching a cricket match – not going on a cross-country run. Shoe full of stones and I've got stung already.

Gary   Half way round the boundary and you're knackered.

Kev   Good job she didn't get in the team.

Gary   Would have needed an oxygen tent after every over.

Kev   He means – kiss of life.

Janet   Where?

Kev   That is a very good question. Answers on a postcard only.

Bill   I was going to offer to be Bondy's runner. But he couldn't afford me fee.

Bill *laughs, but the others don't. They're setting down their bags, taking in the view etc.*

Bill   It's going to be a hot day.

Janet   I hope so. We'll go back as brown as berries.

Bill   Mist over the sea. It'll be very hot once that cloud goes. Temperature in the seventies.

Kev   Thank you Bert Foord. Right, we'll stay here then shall we, for now?

Gary   All right. Drop everything.

Janet   Do you mind?

Kev   Oh yeah, going to be one of them days is it? All innuendo and no bloody action.

He makes a grab at **Janet***, who evades him.*

Janet   Mind, they can see us from the pavilion.

Kev   So what. Give them something a bit more spunky than cricket to watch.

Janet   Here, what's that flashing?

Gary   Binoculars or something, in'it?

Kev   Flash bastards. I bet they never took that much hardware when they climbed Everest. Binoculars, telescopes, cine cameras, sun brollies, car chairs, lilos, picnic hampers – think they're on an expedition to Timbuktu – not a poxy cricket match at Thorpe Bay.

Janet   But I wish we'd stayed over there with them for a bit. Just for the morning, you know.

Kev   What? With them shits?

Janet   We could have had a laugh.

Kev   We'll have a laugh here, won't we.

Janet   You know what I mean, Bill?

Bill   Be like work though. I mean, you can't be yourself with that lot. Specially with their wives and everything with them.

Kev   That's dead right. A day with that lot and I'll end up in a bleeding loony bin. Ears permanently half cocked ready to laugh every time Bondy or Leigh Hunt or Jackson cracks one of their pissy little jokes. Be worse than the bloody coach down here. Ooooo hooooo hooo. Very good, sir.

Gary   Don't know how you do it.

Kev   Quick as a flash. Instant repartee.

Gary   Lightning wit.

Kev   Can't keep up with it. I heard that joke when I was sucking me mum's tits.

Gary   Bad enough in Holborn.

Janet   Never speak to us in Holborn.

Kev   That's another thing. See, they do know our bloody names.

Gary   Right. When we stopped for a cuppa, in the bog. Leigh Hunt was pissing next to me. Says: 'How you settling down in marine, Parker?' Overlooking for a moment that I've been in motor for the past eighteen months, he got me name right. In the office, pass in the corridor, looks at me like I've come to fix a Durex machine in the bog. Bastard.

Kev   All bastards.

Janet   Yeah, but it's different today, in'it. Firm's do.

Kev   Firm's do ought to be in firm's time. Firm's pay.
Not a bloody bank holiday Monday. No charging for the
coach fare either. Assets exceed 267 million pounds. 'Sorry
old boy, gotta charge for the coach. Seventy-five p, pay
Miss Phillpot.' Pill-in-the-pot's making a packet out of this.

Gary   Last year, though.

Kev   You bet. I tell you, there'll be some bloody changes
here once Clive Jenkins starts poking his nose in. There'll
be some bloody changes all right.

Gary   Right.

Kev   Bondy, St John, Jackson, Leigh Hunt – all of them
with the don't-piss-in-the-Windsor-soup voices'll be
demoted to messenger boys. You wait.

Gary   Right.

Kev   No buggering about then with the full weight of
Clive Jenkins behind us. They'll be petrified to try
anything. One out-of-place remark from Bondy, mate, and
everybody out. The whole insurance world will tremble.
They'll be grounding planes, stopping ships and the entire
capitalist world will come to a standstill. Bondy'll be out on
his arse. A vagabond, smoking dog-ends and looking for
scraps to eat in the dustbins.

Janet   Did you see his wife?

Bill   I thought she was his daughter or something.

Janet   No, his wife. I saw her at the Christmas dinner at
the Savoy. She's nice.

Bill   Bloody gorgeous.

Kev   What's she see in a gin-soaked old sod like him?

Gary   Thirty-five grand a year?

Kev   More. Few hundred shares, house in Cyprus he
hires out in the summer. Hand in the till. Still don't know

his arse from his elbow and don't give a fuck whether it shows or not.

Janet   That's what I sorta like about him.

Kev   Like about him?

Janet   Sort of suave, you know. Sort of oozes out of him. 'I'm a snob, a twit and a piss artist. And so what?' Kind of attractive – to some people.

Kev   You better not let Clive Jenkins hear you say that.

Janet   But he knows, don't he. He knows how they all lick his arse, and buy him drinks and – he's taking the piss out of them in a very subtle way.

Kev   There is nothing more disgustingly bourgeois than an excess of subtlety. They should be starting any minute. Know what the team is?

Bill   Bondy opens the batting –

Gary   So they'll have to bowl underarm.

Bill   Then those two blokes out of computers are in, then Winston –

Kev   Is he playing?

Bill   Fourth man. They say he's a good bowler, off spin –

Kev   I know he's a good bowler. He got the chance to sign for Kent. But I didn't think he'd be such a snide shit to play for the firm's team. Didn't no one give him the score?

Gary   He laughed.

Kev   He what?

Gary   Just laughed.

Kev   The patronising nigger. He's only been here a year and he's already playing cricket for bloody Bondy. I'll have to have a word with him.

Gary   Won't make no difference. I told him it weren't the done thing. And –

Kev   And what?

Gary   He just laughed. Said it was stoopid.

Kev   He's let the side down. Very badly.

Janet   Shut up Kev. What would you do if you was asked to play? You'd –

Kev   I'd tell them to go piss up their kilts, mate.

Janet   Yeah?

Bill   Might be different if you *was* asked –

Kev   Listen Billy Boy. The reason they haven't asked me is because I've made it pretty bloody obvious what my answer would be. They hate rejection. It's a sort of allergy they're very sensitive to, due to all the pure inbreeding.

Gary   They asked me to play football for them. When Jackson heard I'd been on Orient's books at school, he tried to get me to play for them. And they play on Wednesdays. Day off every week in the season, it would have been. Trip to Gibraltar at Easter. Talk of going to South Africa, playing the subsidiary there. Laid out the temptations before me they did. I told Jackson what to do with it.

Kev   Good for you.

Bill   What did you say?

Gary   Well, I didn't make it blatant, like.

Bill   So what did you tell him?

Gary   Played it a bit close to me chest. No need to go arousing unnecessary hostility, I thought.

Bill   I see.

Gary   So I told him I'd got a dodgy cartilege and

couldn't play. That was my official reason for declining his invitation. But he knew. He bloody knew all right.

Kev Do all that, all sticking together, and then Winston – just sails off into the cricket team. Betrayed us. Long streak of piss.

Janet If I'm laying here like this, they can see up me legs can't they.

Kev Depends how bored they are by the cricket, love.

Janet Ha-bloody-ha.

Kev *sits*.

Kev Christ. This is bloody lovely isn't it.

Gary I'm sweltering already.

Kev Janet, I'm stone cold sober and I fancy you already.

Janet Ta.

Kev Go swimming in the nude later.

Janet The beach is packed. Like sardines.

Kev Start a new trend, won't we. One year I'm going to go to St Tropez. They sunbathe their tits and no one takes a blind bit of notice. All so natural and healthy and lustful. I'll have to keep a telephone directory on my cock to hold it down.

Bill They're stark naked now.

Kev You what?

Bill St Tropez. They're naked. No costumes. They have lookouts with bugles. When the police come they blow their bugles and everyone puts on their pants.

Kev I don't believe it.

Bill Seen it.

Kev Gerraway.

Bill   I was there in June.

Kev   In St Trop? I thought you was doing your bloody degree exams?

Bill   Afterwards. Mate and me went to France for a couple of weeks.

Kev   Fuck me. Students pissing off to St Trop while we're slaving over a hot accounts book. Tell me you're having me on.

Bill   You sound like my old man.

Kev   I thought you was jobbing at our place to get a bit of money for a holiday.

Bill   That's right.

Kev   Sod me. Where are you going this one? Peking? Miami? Rio de Janeiro? World cruise?

Bill   I'm easy.

Kev   That's nice to know. Glad you're not fussy. What a bloody liberty. Spend six weeks flicking paper clips at Pill-in-the-pot and touching up the canteen girls and then calmly tells us while we're stuck in Holborn for the winter you'll be off to bloody Mexico or somewhere exotic.

Bill *laughs, takes off his shirt.*

Janet   That's what I call a suntan.

Kev   That's what I call a bloody V-sign to the working man.

Janet   What you studying Bill?

Bill   Marine biology.

Gary   Interesting.

Bill   I find it interesting.

Gary   What'll you do afterwards?

Bill   Fish farming – ocean farming. Looking for food under the sea.

Kev   Christ Almighty, that sounds more like a holiday than your bloody holidays do.

Janet   Is it well paid?

Bill   Better be.

Gary   Do you need a degree to get into it?

Bill   Yeah.

Kev   How about for holding your snorkel?

Bill *laughs, sunbathes.*

Gary   What do you think of the office then? I mean, every summer we have students in. Always wonder what they think of it.

Bill   All right.

Janet   You just bugger about all the time. The older ones hate you.

Bill *laughs.*

Kev   The age gap is coming down by the minute. You have bloody got it made, Billy Boy. Haven't been tempted to stay, have you? Make a career in insurance? 'Cause if you have, I'll do a swap with you.

Janet   Anyone fancy an ice cream?

Gary   Yeah, all right.

Janet   Here's ten p – get me one when you go.

Gary   Bloody cheek. What about you Kev?

Kev   One of those runny ones with a lump of chocolate in the middle.

Gary   Bill?

Bill   I'm easy.

Gary   Won't be a tick. (*He goes.*)

Kev   Nice bloke Gary, in't he?

Bill   Seems it.

Kev   He is.

Bill   Happy bloke.

Kev   Bloody right. If he was a bit taller, he'd be earning his crust as a footballer. Orient would have signed him. If he'd been a bit taller. When the Orient didn't sign Gary, his old man never spoke to him for a month. Like it was bloody Gary's fault. Oh Christ! Only another forty years and it'll be like this all the time.

The three lie there: silence for a bit. **Kev**'s *hand starts to climb* **Janet**'s *thigh.*

Janet   I'm watching you, Kev.

Kev   But can you *feel* me, Janet?

Janet   They might be looking through their binoculars.

Kev   So bloody what. Christ, Janet: you are so bloody sexy. (*He rolls on top of her.*)

Janet   Piss off.

Kev   I'm telling you. Everything about you turns me on. Last week, when you was wearing that see-through blouse, I made the Birmingham office's quarter-yearly profit different by a hundred grand every time I added it up. I had to go and have a cold shower. I was in a lather of lust for you. Janet, I'm going to get you bloody drunk today. Helplessly out of control.

Janet   Have you got a girlfriend, Bill?

Bill   Huh huh.

Janet   Oh. Get off Kev, you're bleeding crushing me.

Kev   Let's go down to the beach Janet.

Janet I'm trying to sleep.

Kev After dark. Alone. Just the crushing of the waves and us.

Janet What, and get sand in it and all?

Kev Now that is very revealing. It means –

Janet Oh shut up.

Applause off. **Kev** *walks to the edge of the boundary.*

Kev They're coming out. And they're going to have their photo taken. It'll be in the autumn magazine. Christ Bill – you better put your name down or you won't get a copy.

Gary *enters with the ice creams.*

Gary Leigh Hunt's whites look a nice yellow.

Janet I thought they were his long-johns.

Gary Steaming with Vic chest rub.

Kev Twenty-two blokes out there – and do you know something Bill boy? Not one of them knows the first bloody thing about insurance.

Janet What's all the fuss?

Gary Tossing up to see who goes in first – eh, Christ. None of them have got a coin!

Kev Assets exceed 267 million and – bloody hell.

Janet Do you reckon this grass is a bit damp?

Kev Eh?

Janet Only if it's damp, I better not sit here. See, there's a long history of piles in my family.

Kev I tell you something Janet – I bloody wish you hadn't told me that.

Janet *sits on her bag.* **Kev** *sits beside her again.* **Bill** *sits to one side.* **Gary** *stands bouncing the football on one foot, dribbles etc.*

Gary (*John Arlott voice*)   Essex Division won the toss . . . going in on a good wicket.

Kev   I hope they run up a bloody landslide. See all those blokes there Billy. Know something, son. Not one of them knows a premium from a bloody Irish sweepstake ticket.

Bill   Yeah?

Kev   Yeah. When I first came here . . . couple of years ago . . . heard about this fuss. Great fuss going on. There was this bloke caught screwing a secretary on the boardroom table. Night porter found them.

Bill   Yeah?

Kev   What did they do? Summoned a bloody board meeting. Wheeling them in in their bloody bathchairs . . . Leigh Hunt said: 'The bloke who was screwing her must go. Instant dismissal.' 'No,' said Harrison. 'He's the only chap in the entire firm who can understand the computer.' 'Very well then,' says Leigh Hunt. 'The secretary must go. Instant dismissal.' 'No,' says Mrs Davies. 'She's the only typist in the entire firm that can spell.' 'In that case,' says Leigh Hunt, 'the table must go.'

He laughs and rolls over stroking **Janet**'s *thigh. She is motionless. He moves his hand under her skirt.*

Janet   I'm watching you Kevin.

Kev   But are you feeling me, Janet?

Janet   They might be looking through their binoculars.

Kev   So bloody what. Loosen the cobwebs on their cocks.

Janet   Hark at lover-boy. Some of them old blokes might surprise you. I know. I get invited to all the departmental parties at Christmas.

Kev   I wonder why that might be? I got it – you make the best sandwiches!

Janet   Ha. Oooh, the thicker the carpets, the faster passion throbs through the pin-stripes.

Kev   And the faster out come the heart attack pills.

Janet   You'd be surprised.

Kev   Surprise me then.

Janet   No, better not. I'll embarrass Billy.

Kev   I bet nothing embarrasses Billy, eh. Bloody university. Jammed pack full of non-virgo-intactas with their kaftans and screwed-up skirts, eh. Blue stockings and black suspender belts and chanting Shakespeare's sonnets and smoking pot and fucking like rattlesnakes, eh. That right?

Bill (*reading his book*)   Yeah.

Gary   Those student waitresses at Warner Bros –

Kev   Majorca.

Gary   Under-thirties club. Best of both worlds. All the entertainment of a holiday camp and Spanish sunshine, see.

Kev   Couple of waitresses there was students. Biggest whores on the Costa Brava . . . so I was given to understand.

Janet   Not from personal experience, like.

Kev   Saving meself for you.

Janet   Oh yeah. Mug.

Gary   And he broke his leg –

Kev   Shut your bloody face, Gary.

Gary   Sorry I –

Janet   Oh yeah, forgot about that.

She laughs.

Kev   It wasn't bloody funny –

Janet   No.

Gary   It weren't.

They try not to laugh, but suddenly snort.

Kev   Crutches for weeks. And I had to come in. Doctor wouldn't give me a bloody certificate.

Janet   Tell Billy how it happened.

Kev   The memory is too painful.

Gary   He was so pissed –

Kev   All right, all right.

Gary   He was pissed out of his mind –

Kev   Bloody smell of Bacardi now makes me puke.

Gary   See Bill, we thought – midnight swim. All rushed down to the pool, stripping off as we went – right abandoned – right mad we was – and Kev runs and leaps in the pool, like –

Kev   Stupid Spanish bastards had let out the water. (*Laughter.*) It weren't funny. I could have killed myself. (*Pause. Snorts of laughter.*) There was some disease going round or something. They was on a hygiene kick. No one told me.

Gary   Make you laugh – when his leg was plastered up. Every night we went into the disco . . . they put on the same record . . . must have heard it a thousand times.

Kev   Very humorous are the Spaniards.

Janet   Your theme tune . . .

Gary (*sings*)   'I can't get no-oh – satisfaction . . .'

Janet *and* **Gary**   'I can't get no-oh – girly action and I tried, and I tried . . .'

Kev   All right, all right. Leave it out. Seventy-odd quid that holiday cost. Seventy quid for a half-hundredweight of plaster and a bloody itching leg. (*Pause.*) Apart from that, it weren't so bad. Ever been to Spain, Billy? Lovely country –

Bill   Matter of fact, I was there at Easter.

Kev   Fucking Ada. This Easter?

Bill   Right.

Kev   Jesus. I suppose you do a bit of work now and again for a break, like.

Bill   It was a working trip. Near Alicante, they're doing some very exciting experiments with sea mosses.

Kev   I don't think I've the stomach for that sort of excitement.

Bill   Ten years' time, your stomach'll be full of it.

Kev   I'm sure.

Janet   If you don't mind me asking –

Bill   What?

Janet   How do you afford it?

Bill   The faculty paid – it was very much a working trip.

Kev   I'm very pleased to hear that in no way could it be described as pleasurable.

'Howzat?' and applause off.

Gary   One down, nine to go.

Janet   Winston's bowled him.

Kev   He would. Hey, I think Bondy's touching Winston up.

Janet   Are we winning?

Gary   Only one wicket gone – for five.

Kev   What do you mean *we?*

Janet   I –

Kev   *They're* doing . . . not bad.

Bill   I'm surprised they all take it so seriously.

Kev   Seriously is not the word for it. The IRA could blow up the Stock Exchange, the pound could sink till it drowned and the Queen could turn out to be Lord Lucan in disguise. It still wouldn't be as bad as losing to Essex Division.

Janet *turns onto her stomach.*

Kev   Ooo, Christ Janet. Your arse don't arf turn me on. Pity it isn't where your face is, so we could admire it while you're sitting down.

Janet   You're mad.

Kev   Honest, I'm in a lather of lust for you. I'm going to get you bloody drunk today. Helplessly out of control and then . . . I shall impale you on me penis. (*He dives onto her.*)

Janet   Get off Kev, you're crushing me.

Kev   We'll go down to the beach, Jan.

Janet   I'm trying to get a suntan.

Kev   After dark, alone. While they're all whooping it up at the pavilion dance. We'll copulate with the salt air about our naked bodies, just the sound of lapping waves and faintly in the distance the three-piece band playing the Gay Gordons.

Janet   Oh piss off. You're embarrassing Billy.

Gary   And it's Ansell to bowl, Ansell, renowned throughout Sidcup for his roses, is about to try and prune

Essex Division's batting. Harrr. Stopped at square leg by Winston –

Kev   Bloody Winston. I thought at least he might have had the decency to sabotage the game.

Janet   Do you like cricket, Bill?

Bill   Aye?

Janet   Cricket – do you like it?

Bill   Not bothered.

Janet   I think you're the first student to come to the match. Usually, the students in the summer don't come.

Bill   Experience. The brolly and bowler brigade at play. The pin-stripe brigade letting their hair down. Experience of a lifetime.

Janet   It's tonight they let their hair down. At the pavilion dance. Wait till you see them then –

Bill   Yeah?

Janet   You'd be amazed how they bugger about then . . . really show themselves up . . . Bondy and Leigh Hunt and . . . then tomorrow, at work, just like after the Christmas parties . . . can't meet your eyes . . . right laugh it'll be.

Kev   Pity we ain't going.

Janet   You what?

Kev   No use telling Billy all about it, seeing like that none of us are going to it.

Janet   The dance –

Kev   No.

Janet   You're kidding.

Kev   I'm not. We've got an agreement, love. Them. The shits – we said we'd not have anything to do with them all day.

Janet   But the dance in the pavilion tonight –

Kev   Or that.

Janet   Like hell.

Kev   Nothing to do with them Jan.

Janet   What was the bloody point of coming then?

Kev   Undermine them. Ruin their bloody day for them.

Janet   You're mad.

Kev   All of them over there – all four coach loads . . . they're all looking at us over here and they're saying to themselves: 'What the fuck are they doing over there?'

Janet   What *are* we doing over here?

Kev   We agreed. Getting under their skin. Bloody protesting – having nothing to do with them. Making them bloody uncomfortable.

Janet   And tonight –

Kev   Loads of things we can do. The pier – fairground up the road at Southend. We'll have a great time.

Janet   I'm not buggering off to Southend. I'm going to the bloody dance.

Kev *grips her arm.*

Kev   Jan –

Janet   You're hurting my arm.

Kev   Jan, it's them and us. Got to stick together.

Janet   Let go of my arm.

Pause. He releases her arm. She picks up her bag.

Kev   What you doing?

Janet   Fed up with this . . . bloody stupid. Going with the others.

Kev   But Jan – we're going to have a great day. We've got the beer, we've got the –

Janet   Bye (*She goes.*)

Kev (*shouts*)   When Clive Jenkins gets in here – you'll be out on your arse.

Janet (*off*)   Bollocks.

Kev   Charming in'it.

Gary   She's going.

Kev   Bloody bints. No sense of solidarity, eh.

Gary   No . . .

Kev   Wanted her mirror – flash it in bloody Bondy's eyes when he's batting.

Gary   Still buy one . . . somewhere.

Kev   Makes you sick, don't it, Bill. (*Pause.*) More beer for us. (*He opens a can.*)

'Howzat?' and applause off.

Gary   Second wicket. Two for eleven.

Kev (*quiet*)   If they're not careful . . . we're going to bloody win . . .

Fade.

Scene Two

Lunch break in the match. **Kev** *and* **Gary** *alone.* **Gary** *plays the guitar well and sings two verses of a slow Beatles' ballad.*

Kev   You know something Gary, mate. You ain't got a bad voice.

Gary   Like a blocked up drain –

Kev   Nar –

Gary   Think it's the radiators playing up when I sing in the office –

Kev   Yeah well – singing there, what do you expect. Here, give us – (*He takes the guitar.*)

Gary   Play it?

Kev   At one time – a bit. What's G?

Gary   That there – no there then –

Kev   Never could get me bloody finger there while that one's there. More a pianist's hands, mine.

Gary   Too fat –

Kev   Know what I mean. Not guitar. Too sensitive for the guitar.

Gary   Oh.

Kev   Like falling off a log, musical instruments to some people. Take to them – easy. Aptitude. Still. (*He puts down the guitar.*) Can't be good at everything.

Gary   Right.

Kev   Sort of picked it up, did you?

Gary   Yeah.

Kev   Not learn from books – you can't learn from books. That's how I tried, see. Hopeless.

Gary   Started off from a book –

Kev   But you had a mate who really taught you?

Gary   Oh yeah.

Kev   That's the difference. Great thing to be able to play an instrument. A social accomplishment. Always welcome at parties and that if you can play the old johanna.

Gary   I'll say. Bloke who taught me the guitar – should have seen him on the piano. Christ. No training or nothing. Instinct. Ear. Free drinks in the boozers that had pianos.

Kev   You ought to do something with your singing and that. Guitar. Semi-pro – weekend nights in a pub. Packet there.

Gary   Ain't that good.

Kev   No one's much good. Except the really good ones. You're bloody good.

Gary   Bloke who taught me. Reckoned I was all right. He got up this little band, gigging. Pubs and that. I tried once. By the Elephant – right rough house. Lots of Teds. All they wanted was Sha Na Na and Rockets stuff. First night, bloody fight. Beer bottles chucking – mirror smashed. My mate, the bloke who taught me the guitar, like – just kept playing. I thought, fuck me – there's cool. Know what, he was high. Stoned out of his mind. Like the music, lived for it. Part of gigging, then. I never fancied that.

Kev   Right. You did the right thing. Keep away from that stuff. That's why I never bothered with my band –

Gary   I didn't know you had a band –

Kev   Oh yeah – couple of years ago.

Gary   I thought you couldn't play –

Kev   Drums.

Gary   Arr.

Kev   And sang a bit, you know. But . . . drug scene. Didn't want all that. I quit, got out before they got me. If you're not into drugs, no good. Bit of an outsider, bit of a loner. I didn't want to get involved. Good band though. Good musicians. One of them plays with Elton John's band. American tours, country house and all that. Good mate. But – the price he's paid for it all. He won't see forty.

Gary   Which one's that?

Pause.

Kev   Forget his name. (*Pause.*) I'm like that. End of
chapter. Forget it all. No good keep looking back.

Gary   Right.

Kev   Not like that now, though. I got in at the wrong
time. You ought to give it a try.

Gary   Never fancied it. You know, sort of felt all fingers
and thumbs, lost me voice – in company. Tell you the best
times, when I really liked it . . . With the Orient youth team
. . . great blokes. Like you feel you're all on the way . . .
This one season . . . great team – eight made it, one's had
Under-23 cap . . . this season we had a great run in the
Youth Cup . . . you start travelling a bit when you get past
the fourth round. Until then, all the matches around
London . . . we went up to Birmingham . . . played at St
Andrews – huge – night match, under the floodlights . . .
coming back, just the team and manager and coach in the
team bus . . . won 3–1 . . . great feeling . . . like you're
bigger than everyone else – couldn't sleep that night . . .
feeling so close – like they're all your brothers . . . stopped
at a Chinese on the way out of Brum . . . manager bought
us all great bag of take-away . . . cans of lager . . . coming
back stuffing ourselves . . . talking . . . like in the early hours
of the next morning, like how you talk – real deep . . . got
out me guitar . . . see, I'd taken it on the first match, and it
had become our lucky mascot . . . used to sit in the back of
the coach on the motorway . . . all have this singsong . . .
and I'd play me guitar . . . they was great nights . . .

Long pause.

Best times . . . guitar . . . them nights . . .

Kev   You shouldn't have given up the game, Gary.

Gary   They said I didn't have it . . . me size.

Kev   Fucking stupid reason. Napoleon's too short to join the bloody Territorials . . .

Gary   I knew they was right. When they told me, one Tuesday night, end of the season, April 18th. I knew they was dishing out the Apprentice Pros . . . touch and go . . . and when they told me . . . I went bloody berserk . . . I went . . . Christ . . . but I knew they was right . . .

Pause.

Kev   Still . . .

Gary   Yeah.

Kev *takes a sandwich, eats, drinks his beer.*

Gary   They're taking their time.

Kev   Bloody champagne they have – lunch break, champagne for the team. And their wives. Bloody vile drink. Ulcers, gives you ulcers.

Gary   We had champagne when we got to the semi-finals. In the changing room, they brought in a couple of bottles.

Kev   Lucky you didn't get to the final, mate. Stomach ruined.

Gary   Yeah.

Kev   165 all out. If they had you and me playing – your off-spins and my fast bowling – we'd have scuttled them for a handful of runs.

Gary   I know.

Kev   And *they* know. Bastards.

Bill *arrives from the beach. Jeans rolled up to his knees, shoes in hand.*

Bill   Beach's like the Northern Line. Rush hour.

Kev   Help yourself to a beer, Billy.

Bill   Ta. Not out yet?

Kev   Only need an hour to scuttle this mob. I've seen some bloody bad teams but I reckon my granny and a couple of her mates could have knocked up a better total than them.

Bill   No answer to Winston's bowling.

Kev   Winston's finished. As far as I'm concerned. Winston has had it. He's had his last pint off me. I've got nothing against blacks. I love my black mates like me own brothers. But an educated black is something else. No sense of solidarity with his underprivileged white brothers.

Bill *laughs.* **Kev** *stares hard at him.*

Bill   No Janet then?

Kev   Better not show her face here again today.

Bill   Nor Winston?

Kev   Right.

Bill   You go on like this and –

Pause.

Kev   And what?

Bill   Up to you.

Kev   Right it is.

Bill *gently takes a handkerchief from his pocket, unwraps something and inspects it.*

Kev   What is it?

Bill   Bunodactis verrucosa.

Gary   You what?

Bill   Wartlet. Gem anemone.

Gary   Let's have a look.

Bill Careful – don't touch.

Gary Beautiful . . . really beautiful. Inch long . . .

Bill Just a mass of jelly but . . . see, in the water – (*He puts it in a cup.*) – expanding, like petals . . .

Gary Jesus.

Bill But not a plant . . . carnivorous animal. And they're not petals, but tentacles. About fifty . . . like harpoons . . . any small animal touches them, transfixed and injected with poison and . . . dead. Feel . . . no, won't harm you . . . feels sticky . . . right?

Gary So small . . . See it Kev?

Kev Yeah, I've seen them . . .

Bill Only usually get them in Cornwall or perhaps the south coast . . . strange how it got here. Right out of place.

Kev Tell you something – like to drop that down Janet's knickers –

He goes to take it. **Bill** *puts it back in the cup.*

Bill No. Without water, it'd die.

Kev Janet'll be wetting her drawers later on –

Bill No Kev – leave it.

Kev For fuck's sake. It's only a bleeding anemone.

Bill A special one. Here.

They stare at each other. **Kev** *shrugs.*

Kev And that's what you spend all your time doing is it? Buggering about with them?

Bill You've sussed me. (*He laughs.*)

Kev Better than working for a living.

Gary Not arf.

Kev *glares at* **Gary**.

Gary   Sort of. (*Pause.*) Do you know what I fancy? (*Pause.*) 'I fancy an ice cream.' An ice cream it is. 'Ask the others.' Fancy an ice cream?

Kev   Yeah, all right.

Gary   Bill –

Bill   They'll be melted time you get them back –

Gary   There's a van by the pavilion –

Bill   Okay. Ta.

Gary   Won't be a tick. (*He goes.*)

Pause.

Bill (*strums the guitar*)   Neat. Yours?

Kev   Gary's.

Bill   Play it?

Kev   He does.

Bill   Man of many talents.

Kev   How do you mean?

Bill   Footballer – plays guitar. Nice bloke.

Kev   He is. Bloody nice bloke. (*He lies back, face to the sun.*) Bloody good mate is Gary. We've had some times, I can tell you.

Pause. **Bill** *strums five chords, puts down the guitar.*

Bill   The birds all like him.

Kev   Who?

Bill   Gary.

Kev   Yeah.

Bill   Talk about him, they do. Hear them as you go by

the bog. Aren't they filthy, what they say?

Kev I dunno.

Bill You should listen. An education.

Kev Right up your street then.

Bill Oh yes.

Kev I bet you don't arf take the piss out of us.

Bill Why?

Kev I would. If I was you.

Bill Oh.

Kev (*gets up, restless*) Cousin of mine. Ford's Dagenham. Hundred quid a fucking week.

Bill *whistles*.

Kev Bet you won't get a hundred quid a week.

Bill Doubt it.

Kev Paid for the boredom. Suppose . . . maybe one day . . .

Bill Ford's? Hundred quid a week?

Kev I dunno.

Pause.

Bill Wait till Clive Jenkins gets in.

Kev *grunts*.

Bill Be all right then.

Kev Can you see that lot of . . . shadows . . . letting Clive Jenkins in? Bill . . . they'd rather be machine-gunned by Mick McGahey than have a union card in their pocket. Of their Burton off-the-peg.

Pause.

Day after August bank holiday Monday . . . wearing
grammar school blazer . . . school badge lovingly having
been removed by mother . . . leaving slightly discoloured
shape on the breast pocket, pressed trousers, shiny shoes
. . . Arsenal Supporters' club tie, resembling at ten yards
perhaps a not bad tie . . . reported at reception . . . wearily
shown to lift by contemptuous doorman . . . and up to the
fourth floor . . . where delivered to Mr Charles:
quartermaster and commander-in-chief of army, 400-
strong, male . . . clerks . . . a great sea of shiny arsed, elbow
gleaming, blue serge wearing . . . male clerks . . . hunched
over desks . . . not permitted to smoke . . . clocked in and
out by Mr Charles' severe frown instead of blue-collar
machine . . . some with chairs with arms won by long
service and . . . some with two-square-feet carpets,
functional decoration for . . . something . . . shown to desk
and . . . career launched.

Pause.

Do you have the *News of the World*? Me mum said one
Sunday, 'Here, do you know him?' And I read the story
. . . I'd been off a week with the flu . . . and what I'd
missed! Bloke, forty, grey face, smile sometimes . . . neat,
courteous, ordinary . . . house in Clapham . . . one
Christmas he had a Led Zeppelin album for his son . . .
couldn't picture what his son looked like . . . and there, his
picture in the *News of the World*. Man gone berserk one
Sunday afternoon . . . smashed to pulp the head of his wife
and daughter and then gassed himself . . . the son
discovered it all Monday morning. Such a normal man,
such a nice ordinary decent . . . male clerk . . . occupational
hazard . . .

Pause.

(*His finger in the cup.*) It's changing colour . . .

Bill   They adapt to their surroundings . . . for protection
sometimes . . . sometimes, so they can pounce . . . on
unsuspecting creatures.

Kev   Which one is this?

Bill   Disguises itself . . . hidden in the mosses – so it can pounce. Kill. Survive.

Kev   Gary's taking his time with those bloody ice creams.

Bill   What I can't understand is . . . you staying.

Kev   Me old man's brother wore a bowler hat . . . went to the City . . . had a car. Only bloke we knew who had a car . . . respected man . . . clerk in the city. Me old man, factory – set his heart on me being like me uncle . . . grammar school . . . enough O-levels for clerking but nothing else . . . arrive to discover . . . no money, no status . . . a brothel of seething frustrations and bitterness . . . window-cleaners laughing through the windows at us . . . cunts . . . And yet . . . sufficient education to be . . . outcast from . . . what me mates do . . . educated to be disillusioned? I'm pissed.

Pause. Applause off.

Bill   They're coming out.

Kev   Bondy to open . . . they'll bowl underarm . . .

Bill   Mirror in his eyes?

Kev   Bondy . . . is like Janet says . . . real money . . . style . . . I preserve my hatred for the pissy little clerks who ape Bondy . . . serviette holders and Woolworth's plastic wine-racks and . . . moderation and . . . palates and no bloody appetite . . . mirror in their eyes . . . need a lot of mirrors.

They look at the game.

You watch Bondy, he even bloody bats with a bit of style. Gear all gone yellow – but can see he could play at one time. He'll go for ones so that Winston can do most of the running . . . leg off the back foot – old man's stroke . . . good work.

Bill   Know your cricket?

Kev   Came here – thought sport – could give me a hitch
. . . up . . . (*He lights a cigarette.*) Not in their bloody league . . .
(*He holds his head.*)

Bill   You all right?

Kev   Too much sun gives me a headache . . . forgot me
sunglasses . . .

Enter **Gary**, *he wears cricket whites. Long pause.*

Gary   They . . . was short . . . Leigh Hunt's . . . bit
knackered . . . they . . .

Kev   What?

Gary   Talked me into it . . . somehow . . . I wasn't
thinking . . .

Kev   Sure . . .

Gary   Straight up Kev . . . Seventh man . . . I'll screw
them up . . . make out I'm putting on a show . . . won't go
for runs . . . show what I could do . . . off the back foot,
drives through the gulley . . . but . . . shan't go for runs . . .
seventh column and all that.

Pause.

I better get padded up . . . Got your ice creams . . . (*He goes,
giving the ice creams to* **Bill**.)

Kev *hesitates, then tips the anemone from the cup and stamps on it.
He breathes deeply.* **Bill** *crouches beside it.*

Bill   You can't kill them . . . smash them . . . and they
just grow . . . again . . .

Applause off.

Winston . . .

Kev   Six.

Blackout.

Scene Three

Evening Twilight. Showaddywaddy song, off. Empty stage. Then we hear giggles and mutterings from behind the cricket screen. Then **Janet** *appears – pulling up her knickers and tugging down her skirt.*

Janet   Oh, I do feel better for that. It's like when you're trying to sneeze . . . and someone keeps distracting you . . . makes the eventual sneeze all the better.

Gary *appears, zipping up his jeans.*

Gary   Bloody sneeze!

Janet   You know what I mean.

Gary   Charming. You need a feather not a –

They laugh.

Janet   Could arf do with a drink.

Gary   You're pissed enough already –

Janet   No, something exotic. Not gin. Fed up with gin. Something like sangria. Know it?

Gary   Won the 2.30 at Sandown –

Janet   Sangria . . . that's what I call a drink . . . brandy and that orange spirit, whatever it is . . . and wine. You get it in tall glasses with tons of ice and bits of cucumber and tomatoes –

Gary   Tomatoes!

Janet   Or celery or something floating in it. Oh, it's exotic. We drank that all the time in Lloret. Me and Pauline.

Gary   Old Pauline eh –

Janet   We're going again next month.

Gary   You and Pauline.

Janet   No, I'm going with Pia, 'cause Pauline's getting married, she says, but I dunno . . . You been to Lloret?

Gary No –

Janet (*tuts*)   You ought to go. You haven't been nowhere if you haven't been to Lloret. It's so lovely. Just like a little fishing village . . . with discos, and you can get chips if you ask special . . . and the hotel we go, they have this wine on the table for every meal, as much as you like, and it's all included and nowhere closes till four in the morning and they're arf smart, the boys . . . so lovely the way they treat you . . . and it's all right 'cause they hate the Germans . . . but they've arf got money, and they think nothing of taking you to this open-air disco in the mountains *and* buying you a lovely dinner *and* afterwards . . . (*As if she's just thought of it.*) I wouldn't mind living in Lloret. Last year when I got home I cried for two days . . .

Gary Oh yeah?

Janet · I couldn't wait to get the photos. There was one left over so I got me mum and dad outside the flats and when they come back from Boots me mum said, 'Oooo, what a lovely hotel.' And I said, 'You are daft, that's our bloody flats.'

Gary Ha.

Janet He phoned me every Tuesday and Saturday night.

Gary Who did?

Janet Javeier.

Gary Did he.

Janet He said he was saving up for the ticket . . . to come to East Ham . . . but he never did.

Gary You've got dirt all over your cardigan at the back.

Janet Brush it off then . . . nice of Bondy . . . bottle of champagne.

Gary Good innings I had –

Janet (*smoothing her skirt*)   You can say that again.

Gary   Christ. Kev'll go spare.

Janet   Sod Kev.

Gary   I think he fancies you –

Janet   I don't want you to think I usually do this.

Gary   No –

Janet   Well . . . I think it's the sun . . . after a day in the sun at Lloret . . . oh, it's a different world. You ought to go to Lloret, Gary, really you did.

Gary   I'll come with you and Pia.

Janet   It's all so different out there –

Gary   Different out there. (*He looks at the cricket pitch.*) Didn't mean to but . . . when you're out there . . . and they're coming at you . . . you have to smash them . . . show who's governor . . . score off them . . . put them away . . . smash them . . .

Janet *puts on her shoes, does her lipstick etc.*

Janet   Got a comb?

Gary *gives her a comb.*

Gary   Kev should understand that. Easy to say you'll screw them up but –

Janet   I think I've really caught it today . . . me skin feels all stretched and . . . tingling with the sun. Just the smell of Ambre Solaire reminds me of Lloret.

Gary   I wonder where Kev and Billy are? Do you reckon maybe they went to the dance?

Janet   How should I know?

Gary   He said the Kursaal?

Janet   We'd better get back. I've got my reputation to think of –

Gary   According to form –

Janet   I don't want you telling no one.

Gary   Course not.

Janet   I mean that.

Gary   I know.

Janet   Free agent.

Gary   Right.

Janet   Only young once.

Gary   Course you are.

Janet   Some people enjoy . . . knitting. No one calls them an old bag because they enjoy knitting.

Gary   You what?

Janet   Miss Phillpot . . . I've heard her . . . going on. Know what she needs . . . ought to go to Lloret, be a different woman . . . not that none of the boys in Lloret would be interested in her. Old cow. She likes knitting, I don't look down me nose at her because she does knitting.

Gary   What the bleeding hell you talking about. First it's sneezing and now it's knitting. I've heard of euphemisms, but –

Janet   Do you mind!

Gary   Sorry I spoke.

Janet   Come on then. Might just have the Paul Jones with Bondy. The sun's brought his freckles out. He does look nice with his freckles showing.

Gary   Oh yeah?

They are beginning to go as **Kev** *enters from the other side, more drunk.*

Kev   Halt. Who goes there.

Gary   Kev –

Kev   The conquering hero. Fifty-six not out. Great innings.

Gary   Yeah?

Kev   Through the slips. Three times – six. Great shots. They never covered that.

Gary   Yeah –

Kev   Off the back foot, and all.

Gary   Pitching it –

Kev   Even the googlies – smash, smash, smash.

Gary   You saw –

Kev   I fucking saw all right. (*He grabs* **Gary***, pushes him to his knees.*) What's your game –

Gary   Kev –

Kev   Whose side you on?

Gary   Kev, I didn't mean –

Kev   You didn't mean? Fan-tastic. Fucking fantastic. Fifty-six not out and he weren't trying! This boy will play for England. Janet – this is the greatest kiddo here.

Janet   Why don't you crawl in a hole.

Kev   I can't find one big enough.

Janet   Come on Gary, the tide must be on the turn. There's a funny smell.

Kev   When she talks I see it all in spelling mistakes.

Janet   It's only a game. There's no war going on –

Kev   That's just where you're wrong.

Janet   Am I? What part you playing then? Waiter in the NAAFI?

Kev   Piss off, slag.

Janet   You know what you need Kev? You need a therapeutic fuck.

Kev   Blimey. Where do you get that from? I must start reading *Angélique*.

Gary   Let go Kev . . . please . . . let –

Janet   You want to watch it Gary . . . I think he might be queer for you.

Pause. **Kev** *releases* **Gary**.

Gary   Listen Kev, really I mean –

Kev   Yeah . . . only kidding . . . great . . . I mean, it was good tactics. You showed them . . . I mean, out for a duck . . . that would have been too obvious.

Gary   Right.

Kev   Showed them what we could do –

Gary   Yeah . . .

Kev   If we chose to join them.

Pause. Enter **Bill**.

Kev   Thought you'd drowned.

Bill   Putting back the wartlet . . . needed rocks.

Kev   Coming for a drink then?

Bill   The pavilion?

Kev   Yeah, right Gary?

Gary   Well . . . sure.

Kev   Assets exceed . . . sink some of the profits.

Bill   Free bar?

Kev   Course not.

They go.

Fade. Music: Gary Glitter's 'Alright with the Boys'.

Gotcha

A play in three scenes

Gotcha was first produced on 17 May 1976 at the Soho Poly Theatre Club, London, with the following cast:

Ton   Derek Seaton
Lynne   Polly Hemingway
Kid   Philip Davis
Head   Peter Hughes

Directed by Keith Washington
Designed by Jane Ripley

The setting throughout is the small stockroom in the science department of a large city comprehensive school.

Music

Before the play: Rolling Stones' 'Satisfaction' and 'Street Fighting Man'
Before Scene One: Thunderclap Newman's 'Something in the Air'
Before Scene Two: Rolling Stones' 'Get Off Of My Cloud'
Before Scene Three: The Beatles' 'Here Comes the Sun'
Throughout Scene Three: the slow side of Rod Stewart's *Atlantic Crossing* album
After Scene Three curtain: Rolling Stones' '19th Nervous Breakdown'

Scene One

Thunderclap Newman's 'Something in the Air'. Music fades as lights rise on stockroom.

A spring morning. The blind at the window is lowered. A motorbike dominates the room. **Ton** *enters, a large man wearing a blazer over his football kit. He is smoking. He checks his watch, looks at the bike. He shuts the door, then sits on the bike, making an accelerating noise with his mouth.*

Enter **Lynne**, *attractive, about twenty-five. She carries books and papers. She puts them down, smiles.*

Lynne   America should invade China and drop the atom bomb on Peking. (*She laughs.*) Fourth year . . . their unanimous verdict. McCarthy rules, OK?

Ton *gets off the bike with difficulty.*

Lynne   Hardly ton-up boy outfit.

Ton   The match. Ten minutes, be starting.

Lynne   Someone said, 'It'll take a stud nicely.'

Ton   The pitch, the rain last night.

Lynne   Connotation, word association. A stud. Thought they were talking about you.

Ton   Lynne. This isn't easy.

Lynne   Getting off the bike?

Ton   Last day of term, shan't see you for a few weeks . . .

Lynne   Is that all you wanted to tell me?

Ton (*coughs, stubs out his cigarette*)   I'm nay much of a talker . . .

Lynne   Ideal qualification for a schoolteacher. Quintessential prerequisite for a career in education. I'm nay much of a talker . . .

Ton   Lynne –

Lynne   It's not yours, is it?

Ton   Of course it isn't.

Lynne   What's it doing here?

Ton   No idea.

Lynne   Perhaps it belongs to Raymond –

Ton   He said he thought it was one of the kids'.

Lynne   That's likely. Last day of school, for some of them – before the wide wide world. Final act of defiance.

Ton   Defiance?

Lynne   Motorbikes not allowed in school.

Ton (*lights another cigarette*)   Decided . . . can't go on . . . this deception . . . lying . . . (*Pause.*) Hurting Carol . . .

Lynne   Does she know about us? (*Pause.*) A suspicion?

Ton   She's not stupid.

Lynne   She married you.

Ton   Thanks.

Pause. **Ton** *studies his feet.*

Lynne   So . . . that's it. Fin. Arrivederci . . . dar . . . kaput.

Ton   Well, that's not exactly how I'd have put it . . .

Lynne   But, that's it.

Ton   It's Carol I'm thinking of. And the kids.

Lynne   Oh well, thanks for having me.

Ton   Look, we had . . . some pleasure . . . and – things end.

Lynne   Funny, they do. Everything falls apart. One minute you love someone so badly you could tear out your innards for them. Another day you can pass them in the street and not feel a thing. Okay Ton. (*She sits on the bike.*)

Ton   Look . . . I am sorry.

Lynne   Yes.

Ton   Now somehow . . . feel better, having put the record straight. Weight off my mind.

Lynne   I'm pleased.

Ton   Letting you know where you stand.

Lynne   So . . . for example . . . in the staffroom. Carry on as if nothing happened? I mean – if you're getting stuck on the *Sun* crossword – should I assist or ignore you or – there's no bell.

Ton   It's motorised, they have hooters. (*He sounds the horn.*)

Lynne   So it does. I thought – (*She removes the petrol cap.*) – this . . .

Ton   For Christ's sake! It's the petrol tank!

Lynne   Oh.

Ton   Cigarette burning – up in smoke.

He attempts to stub out his cigarette and replace the petrol cap simultaneously, and **Lynne** *slightly loses her balance; the result is they arrive in a clinch. They look at each other. He kisses her. Then stops.*

Ton   Look, the match –

Lynne   Ton, please, please –

She holds onto him as the door opens and the **Kid** *enters. Sixteen, but looks older. He speaks with a slight stutter not discernible until he is flustered. He is flustered by* **Lynne** *and* **Ton***'s embrace.* **Ton** *glares at the* **Kid**.

Ton   What you doing in here lad?

Pause.

Lynne   I must –

She straightens her skirt. The **Kid** *takes it all in.*

Ton   What are you gaping at? You shouldn't be in here. Out of bounds. What are you doing in here?

Kid   Me . . . bike . . . I . . .

Ton   Yours?

Kid   Me brother's . . .

Ton   Rules, school rules. No motorised bikes. For pupils, not permitted, it's in the rules. And in here. This is a stockroom not the Isle of Man TT.

Pause. Then:

Kid   I . . . I'm leaving today. (*He smiles.*)

Ton   That's no excuse.

Pause. Embarrassment. The **Kid** *is still trying to discover the cause of their embarrassment.*

Ton   You should be out on the playing field – to cheer the staff against the prefects.

Kid   I was . . . going home.

Ton   Not till after the final assembly.

Kid   Oh.

Lynne   I'd better –

Ton   What are you gawking at lad? Hasn't anyone ever told you that it's rude to stare?

Kid   Nar I –

Ton   What are you staring at? Hmmm? And get this damned contraption out of here. Bunsen burners and chemicals and heaven knows what. Tank full of petrol. Go up. Come on, jump to it, chop chop.

The **Kid** *attempts to take the bike but accidentally hits the pedals against* **Ton**'s *shin. He yelps. Then, out of a mixture of fury and embarrassment, he clouts the* **Kid** *round the head.*

Kid   Ah!

Ton   Bloody fool.

Lynne   Ton!

The **Kid** *and* **Ton** *stare at each other; the* **Kid** *holds his head.*

Ton   Bloody idiot. And stop STARING!

Pause. **Ton** *hits the* **Kid** *again, harder.*

Lynne   Ton, for God's sake leave him –

Ton   He's gaping. Open-mouthed moron. (*He lights a cigarette.*) Yes, well . . . seemed to have closed his mouth. So lad, so you're leaving us today? (*Pause.*) Why not till the end of the summer term?

Kid   I . . . I'm sixteen . . . now.

Ton   I see. Look older . . . that your report?

Kid   Yes . . .

Ton   Weak . . . lazy . . . no aptitude . . . very poor . . . lazy . . . Well, you've certainly been consistent.

Kid   Thank you.

Lynne   What arc you going to do?

Silence.

Lynne   What job?

Kid   Dunno . . . (*Pause.*) In here . . . you and her . . . (*He laughs quietly.*) Dirty old –

Ton   SHUT UP.

The **Kid** *sits on the bike.*

Kid   Someone's nicked the top.

Lynne   Here – (*She holds out the petrol cap.*)

Kid   Very . . . d . . . d . . . dangerous. Light a fag over here and – (*He lights a cigarette and laughs at them. He is on the bike, close to the door. He closes the door, turns the key, pockets it.*)

Ton   What the hell –

Lynne   The door –

The **Kid** *waves his cigarette over the petrol tank.*

Kid   Gotcha!

Ton *looks at* **Lynne**.

Ton   Now look here you bloody fool –

Kid   Watchit.

Ton   What's your name?

Kid   Me name?

Ton   What's his name?

Lynne   What's . . . your name?

The **Kid** *laughs.*

Kid   You ask me me name? I've only been here five years!

Ton *goes to him to get the key.*

Ton   Now look here sonny, give me that key.

Kid   Watchit. I'm . . . n . . . n . . . not messing . . . messing. (*He brandishes his fag and* **Ton** *slowly retreats.*) Not, messing.

Lynne   He isn't . . . whoever he is.

Ton   Blow us all up would you?

Kid   Give me one . . . one reason why not?

Pause.

Lynne   Lots of reasons –

Kid   Only asked for one.

Ton   Oh Christ. (*He paces.*)

Kid   Stay still –

Ton   This is ridiculous.

Kid   Still! You make me jittery. When you're jittery, that's when accidents happen.

Lynne   The best way to avoid accidents is to –

Kid   You can shut up and all. (*Pause.*) Fed up getting talked at, in't I. Told what to do, where to go, go there, come here, smash in the f . . . f . . . face. Up to here wiv it. All for – well, that's the end of it. Today. Leaving, right. Five years here, ay. Into the unknown. Nothing . . .

Lynne   Nothing . . . ?

Silence.

Kid   Oh, they've started the football match. STAY!

Ton *has attempted to look out of the window. The* **Kid** *makes him retreat.*

Ton   You really would . . . do that? Have you any conception of the consequences of that action?

Kid   Like what?

Ton   You'd be expelled and no employer would touch you with a shitty fingernail! A lifetime of –

Kid   I thought you'd say – we'll all be killed.

Ton   That, oh yes.

Kid   I doubt even Watling on a bad day'd expel a corpse. 'Look here . . . corpse . . . pull yourself together . . . and take that chewing gum out of yer mouth . . . what I have to say is very serious . . . pay attention . . . look alive . . .' (*He* *laughs.*) Funny smell . . . burning flesh . . . hangs in the air for ages . . .

He looks out of the window. **Lynne** *and* **Ton** *exchange a look.*

Lynne   When you've finished . . . that cigarette . . . we'll all go, shall we?

Long silence.

I said when –

Kid   Fancy screwing him. Great oaf . . . Do you know what we call him . . . Farty. That's what we call him, 'cause he keeps farting in the gym. So we call him Farty.

Ton   You little bastard –

Kid   Suits him, don't you think? Do you know why farts smell? For the benefit of the deaf.

Silence.

Good name, in't it. Farty.

Pause.

Lynne   What's your name?

Kid   I want you . . . I'm telling you . . . From now on, his name, officially is – Farty. Right? (*Pause.*) Say hello to him then. (*Pause.*) I'm warning you!

Pause.

Lynne   Hello Farty.

The **Kid** *laughs.*

Kid   He's done it again! What a stink, what a scorcher! Whenever something makes him mad – he drops one. Cor, that was a terrible one!

Lynne   Awful.

Kid   Diabolical.

Lynne   Appalling.

Kid   Trench warfare – secret weapon – him.

Lynne   Oh yes. (*She laughs.*)

Ton   All right, Lynne . . . no need to . . . (*To the* **Kid**.) Look here, that's enough. The game has gone on sufficiently to satisfy your end-of-school high-jinks, now I propose –

Kid   Farty!

Ton   Listen, they're waiting for me out there. I've got a game of football to play. I'm right half!

Kid   Ooooo.

Ton   Miss Millar, I –

Kid   Gorilla.

Pause.

Lynne   What?

Kid   Gorilla Millar, your name.

Ton   Ha ha.

Silence.

Kid   Good, in't it.

Ton   Oh –

Kid   Say hello to each other then. (*Pause.*) Go on, don't be shy. (*Pause.*) I ain't fucking joking!

Ton   Hello, Gorilla.

Lynne   Hello, Farty.

The **Kid** *giggles, snorts, holds himself.*

Ton   There, satisfied? Now can we please go?

Kid   Oh no. Not yet. I mean to say, satisfied – well, satisfied is hardly the way I'm feeling. A very wrong word to use is satisfied. (*He looks out of the window.*) They've started the game without you Farty. Jenkins must have taken your place. The Billy Bonds of Botany.

Ton   They'll be looking for me. Watling will have sent out search parties. My God, I'd hate to be in your shoes when they find you.

Kid *(laughs again, turns to them)*   In't it funny. Eh? What a scream. Farty is . . . scared. I can see it. Scared of me. You're sweating top of yer mouth . . . Forehead all red and thundery and . . . Years of shoving everyone around, slapping heads in the corridor, getting us giddy in the gym and doing everything you like and now – Shitting yourself 'cause I got the power. Ain't I.

Ton   You little . . . turd.

Kid   Oooo, Betty. Naughty word . . . naughty . . . not nice.

Ton   Shall I tell you why you're such a . . . stupid little sod, whatever your name is. Because you're short-sighted. That's why you're so stupid.

Kid   That ain't my fault.

Ton   Of course it is.

Kid   I can't help it.

Ton   Yes you can.

Kid   Can't.

Ton   Can.

Kid   I can't help it, can I, Gorilla?

Lynne   No . . . you can't help being stupid.

Kid   Thank you. See.

Ton   But you can help being short-sighted. You don't look further than your feet. Do you? Just look as far as your feet carry you. Live from day to day –

Kid   I never plan that far ahead.

Ton   You think you can call me . . . that word . . . and
Miss Millar –

Lynne   That word.

Ton   Quiet, woman. Well, big laugh, very funny, oh ho
ho. But, but what afterwards, hmm? The consequences.
What then?

Pause. The **Kid** *lights a cigarette with hypnotising slowness.*

Kid   What after today for me . . . anyhow . . . I've been
here, getting prepared for today for . . . five years. The
great day. Stepping out into the wide wide world, an' that.
One of . . . how many kids here? Twelve hundred, eh.
What's going to happen to this one here – (*He points at
himself.*) – after today? Hmmm? Mmmm? Fifty years of
working life is . . . all spread out in front of me . . . they say
when you drown, in the last seconds before you go under,
the whole of your life passes before your eyes . . . Well, this
morning as we all stood there in the assembly, and the
choir sang them hymns and the brass band blowed on
their bugles and those clever bastards chanted out their bit
of rhyme in Latin, an' that . . . and the mayor made his
speech, so proud, so proud . . . and we all said them
prayers to God Almighty . . . and we watched all them
clever kids getting their prizes . . . clapping, clapping . . .
going to university . . . clapping clapping . . . playing
cricket for England. Boys in Pakistan . . . clapping
clapping. . . well, me life didn't pass in front of me eyes . . .
but me future did. A great mist of nothing . . . (*Silence. He
lights a cigarette. Looks out of the window.*) Pigeons sitting on the
power cables . . . got it made, ain't they . . . can sit on
power cables and not get burned . . . fly anywhere . . .
Grandad had 'em . . . funny, in't it . . . how pigeons don't
sweat under their wings when they've been flying . . .

Pause.

Ton   What do you want?

Kid   Bonny! Want Bonny up here . . . in front of me . . .
up here, down there . . . knees . . . make him sweat, make
him bleed . . . blow him up! Know why he's called Bonny?
'Cause he keeps –

Lynne   Asking everyone if they're *bona fide*?

Kid   Right! Noticed that an' all? Noticed that, first thing
I noticed when I came here, this lovely comprehensive.
Him going up to the sixth formers and saying: Are you
bona fide – 'bout university? About cricket tour, are you *bona
fide*? I thought: 'Christ, what a lot of fucking brothers.' And
then someone says, 'Nar – Latin, in't it. Means, serious.'
An' I thought – told me brother and he said: 'Great school
great school, going round talking in Latin all day.' Great –
that's the way to get your head smashed in in the factory, I
think. (*Cool now.*) I want him, here. Bonny. I'm serious. See
him?

Ton   Yes . . .

Kid   Call him then, go on!

Ton (*at the window*)   Mr Watling. Headmaster.

Kid   Bonny!

Ton   Yes, ah – up here. The science stockroom.

Kid   Close it.

Ton *closes the window.*

Kid   He coming?

Ton   Yes . . .

Kid   Well, in't this nice and cosy?

Blackout. Crash in Stones' 'Get Off Of My Cloud'.

Scene Two

Music continues, fades out before lights come up.

*Knocking on the door. Lights up to reveal: the **Kid** on bike; **Lynne** and **Ton** anxious. The knocking continues.*

Voice (*off*)   Mr Peart, are you there?

*The **Kid** nods that **Ton** should reply.*

Ton   Yes, I'm here.

Voice (*off*)   Then, open the door.

Ton   I . . . I'm . . . we're in a bit of a jam.

Pause.

Voice (*off*)   A what?

Ton   There's a kid here – gone berserk.

*The **Kid** laughs.*

Voice (*off*)   Who's there?

Kid   Listen Bonny. D'yer wanna come in?

Voice (*off*)   Open this door.

Kid   Ask nicely.

Voice (*off*)   OPEN THIS DOOR IMMEDIATELY.

*The **Kid** giggles.*

Kid   Well, if you ain't gonna ask nicely, you ain't gonna come in. Fair's fair.

Voice (*off*)   What is going on in there?

Ton   We're . . . sort of hostages.

Voice (*off*)   Who is with you?

Ton   Miss Millar and – a lad.

Voice (*off*)   Who is it?

Kid (*whispers*) King.

Ton (*loud*) His name is King.

Kid Arthur.

Ton Arthur. (*He glares at the* **Kid**, *who laughs.*)

Voice (*off*) Open this door at once!

Kid Say please.

Ton I think, headmaster –

Lynne It does appear . . . serious.

Pause.

Voice (*off*) Let me in . . . please.

Kid I can't hear him, can you?

Ton I –

Kid Louder, Bonny. Farty here's breathing so heavy I can't hear you.

Voice (*off*) Please. Let me in.

Kid Please.

Voice (*off*) Please.

Kid Coming to something when I have to teach a headmaster his manners, like. Didn't no one teach you no manners? Still can't hear you, tell you what . . . gap under the door. Talk through that – might hear yer then.

Voice (*off*) Wait there Mr Peart – I'll get the caretaker, master key –

The **Kid** *holds his cigarette closer to the petrol tank and screams.*

Kid I ain't fucking joking!

Ton You fool – close to the fumes – get it away from the fumes – don't you know too close to the fumes and, accidentally –

Kid   Makes it exciting, dunnit! Get him in here. I want him in here.

Lynne   I think, headmaster . . . before things slip out of hand –

Ton   Tragedy –

Lynne   It would be best if you do what –

Kid   King Arthur –

Lynne   Says.

Pause.

Voice (*from the gap under the door*)   Please let me come in.

Pause.

Kid   Right. Action stations. Put out the red carpet – stand to attention, hats off for the Queen. (*He gestures* **Lynne** *to stand close to him. He holds her hair above the tank with one hand and the cigarette with the other.*) Him in. You try anything and I ain't kidding – we're all blood and bone on the ceiling, right! (*He puts his hand up* **Lynne***'s skirt.*)

Ton   You filthy little bastard.

Kid   What does it say on Durex machines?

Ton   I –

Kid   Shut up.

Lynne   I don't know. What does it say on Durex machines?

Kid   Buy me and stop one. Heeeeee. Oh, that's nice . . . exciting.

Ton *rages.*

Kid   So what. I'm in charge now Farty. Your time is up. Go dance on . . . go crunch eggshells now. Here's the key. Open up and let him in and lock it and key back to me and try anything and I break a bottle in her cunt. Right.

This is done gingerly. The door opens and we find the headmaster on his knees. He enters.

Head   Oh, I see . . .

Kid   Shut it. Door.

Ton *shuts the door, gives the* **Kid** *the key. Silence. The* **Kid** *gropes her more.*

Head   Remove your hand. I take your point.

Kid   Bollocks. She likes it. (*Then he releases her. She wipes her watering eyes. Adjusts her dress.*)

The three adults look at each other.

Head   I have no idea what precisely you think you are playing at, but I give you warning, the repercussions are going to be exceedingly serious.

Kid   *Bona fide?*

Pause.

Ton   He's, he's – threatening to.

The **Kid** *lights a cigarette.*

Head   There is a very strict rule in this school preventing pupils smoking on the premises.

Kid   Nice one.

Ton   He's threatening to . . . set off the petrol.

Kid   Right.

Lynne   Please . . . please . . .

Head   What do you hope to . . . what do you think you're going to achieve by this? Err, Johnson isn't it?

Kid   No.

Head   Raynor –

Kid   No.

Head Ansell –

Kid Pass.

Pause.

Head Do you know him?

Ton I think . . . I've seen him about the school.

Head Miss Millar?

Lynne I recognise . . . him, but –

Head Neither of you know his name?

Lynne No.

Head I see.

Ton It's an . . . awfully big school, headmaster –

Head I am aware of that.

Ton Can't be expected to know the names of all twelve hundred –

Head I am interested only in *his* name. Well, boy? This has gone on far long enough. What's your name?

Kid It's on me report.

Ton Ah yes! He had his report.

Head He's shown it to you?

Ton Yes.

Head What name was on it?

Pause.

Ton Ah, I didn't actually notice –

Head And you, Miss Millar?

Lynne No, I didn't.

Pause.

Head   Okay lad. Let's see it. If you are not prepared to tell us your name, let me read it –

Kid   No.

Head   I see no –

Kid   No. It's mine. My property. I mean, like the way I gathered . . . this report here in me pocket, it's what I show the employment exchange, an' that – to get a job. And all them things you lot . . . teachers . . . written on it. Well, way I see it, none of them didn't exactly do me a favour. None of that gonna help me much – specially what *you* wrote. Headmaster's comment, at the bottom, God's word, the big deal the final sentence, end of trial – judge's verdict. (*Pause.*) Achieved little here . . . not a success . . . (*Pause.*) That's what you wrote, an' signed it an' – (*Slight pause.*) An' now you tell me you don't know who the fuck I am!

Silence.

Head   Then you tell me who you are.

Kid   Ahhha. Listen, way I see it, I reckon you oughta found out who this geezer here was before you started putting in the boot. Not a success, weak, lazy, no aptitude, no achievement an' – lovely signature though.

Head   I cannot reasonably be expected to know everyone here. I have to rely upon the opinions of the other members of my staff . . . who do know the pupils.

Kid   What, him? Farty there? He don't know me from Adam. And her? She don't know me. An' you don't. I'm the only bleeder here who knows who I am!

Head   This is all . . . rather beside the point.

Kid (*to* **Lynne**)   Give us a kiss.

Lynne   I'd rather not.

Kid   If you play your cards right, I'll let you have a suck.

Head   This . . . gratuitous crudity –

Kid   Kissus.

Lynne   Let me see your report first.

Kid (*in a child's voice*)   If I show you my report will you show me what's under your knickers?

Ton *has moved towards him.*

Kid   Hold it, Farty – far enough, no more! Christ, how many more times! I ain't kiddin' you know! This is . . . for real. This is, it. Ever seen what happens when you walk through a fire?

Pause.

Head   Was all this . . . a premeditated rebellion?

Kid   You what?

Head   Was all this – premeditated?

Kid   Come again?

Head   I asked –

Lynne   Did you plan this?

Kid   Oh. (*He lights a cigarette.*)

Head   If it was unplanned, let us stop it now and forget all about a momentary lapse . . . a slight madness of the moment.

Kid   Oh . . . Oh . . . runs in the family. Me grandmum was mad. Ol' Grandma. Round the bleedin' bend, she went. They locked her up. In a room no bigger than this. I used to go and see her. She sat in the garden. And peeled chestnuts and buried orange pips in the grass. I said to her: 'Why are you here?' She said: 'They say I'm mad.' I said, 'Why's that?' She says: ''Cause I go up the shops with no clothes on.' I said: 'Don't you feel cold?' 'Nar,' she says, 'I only do it in heatwaves.'

Pause.

Lynne   You liked her?

Kid   Me gran?

Lynne   Yes. . .?

Kid   Course I did, everyone loves their grans.

Lynne   Did she die?

Kid   Mind your own.

Lynne   Just interest.

Kid   She used to wet the bed . . . they had to take her away. She kept wetting the bed.

Lynne   Was she very old?

Kid   Dunno . . . She seemed a hundred, but I was younger. She said to me brother: 'If you ain't in bed by ten o'clock, come home.' (*He laughs.*)

Lynne *laughs; the* **Kid** *laughs more. The* **Head** *laughs;* **Ton** *makes out he is laughing. Slowly, they stop laughing.*

Kid   I never got it.

Pause.

Ton   This is all fantastically interesting but isn't it about time –

Head   Jolly interesting indeed. Your grandmother sounds a most remarkable woman.

Kid   You should have heard her sing!

Head   I would . . . very much like to have heard her sing.

Kid   Duke's Head, that's where she sang.

Head   Ah, in the High Street –

Kid   An' played the piano. Johanna. She had this johanna at home. An' every Christmas, when we was kids,

we'd go there and she'd play the johanna. An' every
Christmas, just before Christmas, she'd paint it – you
know, with that wood-dye stuff an' then the room'd hot
up, you know, everyone there, singing an' that. And me
old man'd say . . . Well, see – he'd put his beer glass on top
of the piano while they was all singing an' that – and all
the fellahs'd try and get their glasses off the piano – (*He
mimes it.*) But – they'd have been stuck there 'cause the
wood-dye was tacky, you know! Laugh!

Head Home entertainments.

Kid Yeah.

Head Rarely one hears a piano nowadays.

Kid Except in assembly.

Head Not the same thing.

Kid It ain't.

Head Not like the self-entertainment of closely knit
working-class families, the simple pleasures, the warm feel
of –

Kid She stopped wetting the bed.

Head An advancement –

Kid An' shit in it instead. So, they locked her up. (*Pause.*)
Stupid thing to do. The lav was a half mile walk away.

The **Head** *is passing a message with his eyes to* **Lynne** *during all
this, as the* **Kid** *looks out of the window.*

Kid Close, should have scored. The prefects' keeper –
he's a wanker. Talk about let a ball through his legs – a
bleeding oil tanker could get through his legs.

Head Are you all right, Miss Millar?

Lynne Just a bit . . . claustrophobic.

Head You look . . . unwell . . .

Lynne It's . . . my time, you know.

Head   Ah, you had better – sit down . . .

Lynne   Yes, I –

Head   Mr Peart –

Ton   Oh. Yes –

Head   The stool for Miss Millar –

Ton   Ah –

Head   I think she's going to faint –

During the confusion of **Lynne** *staggering and* **Ton** *getting the stool and passing it to the* **Head**, *the* **Kid** *loses his concentration, and* **Ton** *makes a grab for his cigarette. But the* **Kid** *knocks* **Ton** *off balance and screams.*

Kid   YOU TRICKING BASTARDS! Right. You've fucking had it now. Stay there Farty, don't get up, lay down. That's it. Right. Okay. Fags outa pockets, right. Fast. I'm warning you.

Ton *removes his cigarettes.*

Kid   An' yours.

The **Head** *slowly hands him his cigarettes – across the floor.*

Kid   Right. (*Panting, wipes his forehead.*) Stay . . . stay there Farty.

Ton   This is – insanity!

Kid   No one's asking you.

Ton   Madness.

Kid   You should know, you're a bleeding loon.

Ton   If you aren't careful, your stupidity will become a severe handicap to you.

Kid   Shut up! Stop . . . m . . . m . . . mixing me up. I'm . . . I'm all on me own up here!

Silence.

Understand that.

Ton   I understand all right, Sonny Jim. All of you – all endless provocations!

Kid   Bastard!

Ton   Little shit.

Kid   An' you can stop laughing an' all.

Lynne   I'm not laughing . . . I'm not. I feel . . . sad for you, your loneliness.

Kid   I got hundreds of mates. Send 'em up here, I will. Do you over.

Lynne   Yes. I deserve it, I'm sure.

Kid   Dirty trick, that was – filthy, disgusting.

Lynne   I do . . . feel faint.

Kid   You said you was on.

Lynne   I do feel faint.

Kid   Bit different. Have you doing handstands.

Lynne   Why not cartwheels?

Kid   Not enough room, or I would.

Lynne   Shame.

Kid   Preaching morality at us. . . all day. What to do. Having it off with this pig here. Married, in't he. That's not what you teach us.

Lynne   I don't think it is really any of your business.

Kid   I see right through you.

Lynne   You don't have to be . . . alone.

Kid   Don't try an' butter me up –

Ton   Waste of bloody butter.

Kid   Okay Farty, keep you quiet. Fifty press-ups.

Ton   Fifty!

Kid   Fifty!

Ton   I'm not doing no fifty –

Kid   You made Henry do fifty and he had a boil under his arm.

Ton   Ah, so you're one of Henry's mob are you? The choc ice and vinegar crisps luncheon club.

Kid (*kicks him*)   Move.

Ton   If it makes you feel very big . . . (*Begins press-ups.*)

Head   I'm . . . sorry.

Pause.

Kid   That's better.

Head   I meant, I'm sorry but I simply don't understand what you are hoping to achieve.

Kid   Ah ha. Ha ha. I've heard that one before.

Head   What –

Kid   Don't tell me, I'll get it . . . it'll come to me . . . achieve . . . achieve – I know! The school motto!

Head   The what?

Kid   No, your signature tune? Yeah! Okay, I don't get it. Give us another clue.

Head   What are you talking about?

Kid   Here, in this place, everyone's so busy ACHIEVING, everything else is . . . invisible.

Pause.

Lynne   I think he is trying to say . . .

Kid   What am I trying to say?

Lynne   Do you mean –

Kid   You've got . . . terrific eyes, you know . . .

Lynne   Are you saying, your apparent . . . lack of success at school –

Kid   Success! That's the other word, like that word . . . knocks me out that word. Oh here – there's a lot of it about.

Lynne   And you . . . sense an awareness . . . that you have been unable to compete on those terms although –

Kid   What the bleedin' hell are you talking about darling?

Ton *stops doing press-ups.*

Ton   Don't humour the sod, Lynne.

Kid   Keep your arse down Farty, I can see your brains moving.

Ton   Headmaster, really – isn't it about time that –

Kid   I said, fifty.

Ton   I did fifty.

Kid   No, you never.

Ton   You weren't counting.

Kid   Start again, an' I'll count this time.

Ton   That's not fair!

Kid   Too bad.

Ton   I've had enough of this.

Kid   Your hard luck.

Ton   Listen boy, when this little game is over –

Kid   Oh yeah, go on go on go on, tell me!

Ton*'s rage becomes hysterical.*

Ton   When you've burned your silly little weedy fingers with your silly little matches –

Kid   Whey, hey!

Ton   Then I shall be fully entitled to do what normally I am not permitted to do –

Kid (*holds his nose*)   Cor, what a scorcher!

Ton   You are the basest –

Kid   Open the bull gates –

Ton   Snivelling, snot-stained –

Kid   Fight! Fight!

Ton   There is a stench of second-classness in this room which is positively nauseating. Everything about you – puny, spotty, skinny –

Kid   Oi oi.

Ton   Second-class, second-rate – that's you. No-bloody-hoper.

Kid   I like it. I like it.

Ton   There's only one thing this sort of herbert understands –

Head   Really, Mr Peart, control yourself!

Ton   You can't argue with them, headmaster. You can't be rational with the irrational –

Head   Mr Peart, you are not helping the situation!

Ton   I am not interested in helping yobboes like this one. I am interested in decency and endeavour and – order. He is disorder.

Head   Let us talk –

Ton   But it's a waste of time talking to someone like him.
Words don't have meaning with people like – Kung Fu in
the playground and sick-notes on the playing field. He can
only mock, he cannot do. And whine and complain. And
leer. Look at him, headmaster. Leering. Make no mistake,
headmaster, that is a leer if ever I saw one, a chromium-
plated leer.

Kid   I'm only here for the leer.

Ton   Little shit. No good wasting words on him; not a
word in the ear of this one, only thing he'll understand is a
kick in the balls, mate. (*Screaming.*) He's the sort of boyo
who's never done fifty press-ups in his life! And . . . he's
scared, oh yes, scared, scared . . . more terrified than he's
ever been in his life, because this time he's gone too far . . .
too, too far and he knows it and he's terrified.

Pause.

Kid   But I ain't the one who's shaking. (*He laughs, slightly
hysterically.*)

Ton   Go on, laugh, laugh. That's all you can do. Mock,
snigger, and whine afterwards. That's you, I know you.
The shadows who never have showers, never do games,
never do anything except march round the school in
gangs, kicking doors, disrupting lessons, picking fights and
jeering outside the staffroom. Do you know what you
need? You need castrating! If you had any sense you'd
know what castrating means and so you wouldn't laugh.
Because in a little while you'll be babbling incoherent
apologies at my knees and I'll kick your fucking head in!

Silence.

Kid   Finding out m . . . m . . . more a . . . b . . . b . . . bout
him than me. Oh . . . suddenly . . . feel brass monkey . . .

Lynne   You're shivering . . .

Kid   Cold in here . . . sudden, all of a . . . cold . . .

Lynne   Let us go out, out into the sun.

Kid   Gives me headaches, sun . . . don't like the sun, much . . . runs in the family . . . 'Welcome to the Birds'-Eye country . . . '

Lynne   What's that mean?

Kid   Summer adverts . . . fields an' flowers an . . . summer pisses me off, you know.

Pause.

Head   Would you mind awfully if I had a cigarette?

Kid   What was that?

Head   I said –

Kid   Funny noise. Are the radiators playing up? Could have sworn I heard sommat.

Head   I said would you –

Kid   You still here. Christ. Still! You know, you're onto a winner here. Other jobs, factories an' 'at – missing five minutes and they dock yer pay. You been here half an hour and no one realises you've been gone.

Head   Oh, they will.

Kid   Reckon?

Head   I most certainly do.

Kid   I don't. I reckon everyone's having a so lovely time. No you pacing about the corridors, hammering doors, disrupting lessons and kinda picking fights. Sticking yer hooter in where you ain't welcome.

Head   May I . . . please? . . . have one of my cigarettes.

Kid   Ah, oh no . . . no chance. I mean, might need that one. The one I give you might be me last one. Saving it, for the big bang.

Head Very well then. Perhaps you will . . . at least
enlighten me. What is this all about?

Kid I ain't messin' about.

Head I believe you. You have convinced me of that.
But, I would very much like to know what –

Kid Come in here, for the motor – saw them, at it. Oh,
got this pain in me head . . . behind me eyes . . . started!
This . . . did . . .

Head An unpremeditated chain of events began which
. . . will end where?

Silence.

Well?

Kid D . . . d . . . dunno, sir.

Silence.

Don't ask me questions . . .

Head Then think about it. We can't stay here for ever.
Soon, you'll be getting hungry.

Kid No trouble. Shout out the window. Tell them to
send in food for us. Tons of it. Anything we want, they'll
send it in. Like the Balcombe Street thingy. From the cafe,
piping hot. Chips an' that. Soup. Surprised the old-age
pensioners ain't started it. Say they're held prisoners in
their flats an' that. Get the cops to rush 'em up grub. Cut
the cost of living, they'd live like kings. No charge, see.
Chicken and chips an' –

Lynne Roast beef!

Kid Oh yeah, an' tons of spuds –

Lynne Roasted –

Kid No way different. Lamb chops and sausages an' hot
dogs –

Lynne   Pizzas –

Kid   Salami and onion, pepperoni special –

Lynne   Don't get that school dinners.

Kid   You're making me feel hungry.

Lynne   I am.

Pause.

Kid   What you doing with a nutter like him?

She shrugs.

'Cause, you ain't so bad-looking.

Pause.

Lynne   Too skinny.

Kid   Nar, just right.

Lynne   Bones, all bones.

Kid   It's the right look now.

Lynne   No. (*She gestures towards her breasts.*)

Kid   Overrated, them are . . . as long as there's sommat there.

Lynne   Oh, they're there –

Kid   That's all right then.

Lynne   Not much but –

Kid   Bums.

Lynne   Beg your pardon?

Kid   Bums. Bum man, me.

Ton   Bloody queer.

Kid   You can shut up. I've had enough of you, Peart, I'm talking to the lady. So . . . you like bums?

Head I . . . do not dislike them.

Kid Herrrrrrr.

Slight pause.

Lynne Do you have a girlfriend?

Pause.

Kid Ah ha.

Lynne All right, I'm sorry. It has nothing to do with me.

Kid Make you laugh, years ago this was, me brother got sent home from junior school with a letter saying he'd been sent home for touching up Peggy Highsmith's tits. Me dad, this was when he was living at home, see – he says to Roy: 'That's really disgusting Roy, I'm ashamed of you. When I was your age I'd have had me hands in her quim.' (*He laughs.*)

Ton You'd need a bloody compass, to find it.

Kid If he don't shut up I'll lip him.

Ton Oh yes? I doubt it. But I do know that I'm going to take that cigarette out of your hand –

Kid Then you'd better move fast Farty. (*He holds it over the petrol tank.*) Okay. This is it. Count of ten. Ten, nine, eight, seven, six, five . . . say yer prayers . . . four, three, two, one –

*The **Head** faces the door. **Lynne** closes her eyes. Then **Ton** closes his eyes. The **Kid** drops a huge rack of test-tubes on the floor. Smash! He screams with laughter. Slowly, they recover from their fear.*

Lynne Very clever. Very good, very convincing. Sure fooled us.

*The **Kid** lights a new cigarette.*

Kid Yeah.

Head   You have made a . . . point of sorts. What do you want?

Kid   What a question!

Head   I'm sorry if it appears perverse, but –

Kid   Watch your bleeding language.

Head   What is all this . . . spectacle . . . supposed to mean?

Kid   You're twitching.

Head   Ah.

Kid   A definite twitch.

Head   I'm getting rather tired.

Kid   You've got rather a long day. Match this morning, end of term assembly this afternoon and dance for the sixth form tonight, their dance, don't forget that.

Head   What do you want of us?

Kid   Oh yeah, a lot of talking you've got on today. Oh yeah. One thing I've always wondered – you don't mind me asking do you? Well, I've always wondered – do you get as bored talking as we do listening?

Pause.

Head   Mr Peart, as you are nearest to the window, perhaps you'd try to raise the alarm.

Ton   Ah, yes.

Kid   Oi –

Head   But I presume this entire drama is some obscure attempt to draw attention to yourself . . . Thus, by raising the alarm, Mr Peart will be assisting in your cause.

Kid   You don't arf get on me tits when you talk like that.

Head   Like . . . what?

Kid   Bored . . . weary voice . . . you know, seen it all
before . . .

Head   As a matter of fact, I do rather find all this . . .
boring. It's a waste of time.

Kid   My five years here have been a waste of time.

Lynne   Have they?

Kid   For a teacher, you can't arf be thick.

Lynne   I do my best.

Kid   It ain't fucking good enough!

Head   For . . . you?

Kid   Don't be smug, Bonny, don't sneer, don't piss all
over me. A couple of minutes ago you was shitting
yourself.

Head   You are deluding yourself, boy.

Kid   I could see it . . . in your eyes . . . I can see what you
think. It's in your eyes . . . First day here . . . lined up in
front of you, all hundreds of us – the new kids. Lined up in
the playground . . . all of us in lines and you wandering
along, eyes flickering over us . . . deciding who's doing
what, who's going where. Flick of the eyes . . . he's got a
nice jacket. Clean trousers and starched handkerchief . . .
O-levels for him. Like Farty says, you see the no-hopers
. . . relegate them. Out of the way.

He takes a long drag on his cigarette.

Listen to your chat, speech-day – mayor there . . . talking.
About how proud he is of this school, this everso terrific
comprehensive school . . . the big, big, school . . . everyone
all together . . . all chances, hundreds of subjects,
something for everyone, put out your hand and take what
you want – But . . . watched your eyes . . . not even looking
at the poor sod of a mayor. 'Humour him,' your eyes said.
'Humour him. Dreamer!'

He sighs. Pause.

Now . . . found out . . . I was right. Comprehensive! (*He spits.*) Me brother, me brother wow, what he said about it when I come here! Chance for you, kiddo, he said to me. Secondary school he went to. No hope. Chucked in there. Factory fodder, but this comprehensive! Paradise. So different he said . . . and he supposed to know. Knows the mayor, delivered his leaflets for him at elections, me brother did. Knew all about what was gonna happen in this new school. This is your big chance, kiddo, he says . . .

Pause.

Got it wrong. Just the same. Only bigger. Anything you want here, they said. Yeah. If you're clever, if you're bright, big hope . . . glittering prizes! Just the same, as it was for me brother . . . just . . . the same. Only bigger. Achievement . . . successes . . . only way it's judged . . . all them O-levels, all them A-levels, all them clever bastards going to university. What a clever headmaster, what a smashing lot a teachers, what a great school. What a fantastic school – What about us? Who don't do O-levels? What about me, eh? How good is this?

He throws the report on the floor. Stamps on it. Stands breathing deeply.

Head   It is . . . never easy to build a perfect world . . . a new Jerusalem in Rainham . . . It's a gradual process, slow steps . . . making a net of tighter mesh . . . it takes time.

Kid   Time, I do not have. Only . . . one life.

Head   Even so, every opportunity has been afforded to you here. If you have some grievance –

Kid   You don't even know me name!

Head   You won't tell me.

Kid   You should find out.

Head   You must help yourself.

Kid   That's your get-out, in't it. Help yourself – help yourself – and if you *can't* help yourself – then it's your own fucking fault.

Pause.

Lynne   What do you want to do?

Kid   He said . . . they all said here – EVERYTHING's possible. On the threshold of . . . everything you want.

Lynne   What do you want?

Kid   Bit late in the day . . .

Head   For God's sake – you're only sixteen.

Kid   Still time?

They are encouraged by this change of tack.

Head   A lifetime before you . . .

Kid   Do . . . anything . . . aye?

Head   Within your capabilities.

Kid   I thought the idea here was to 'expand' them.

Head   Yes, yes – that is the premise upon which –

Kid (*waving his cigarette near the petrol*)   I wanna blow you up, *Bonny*.

Head   Mr Peart, are you having any –

Kid   Wanna see you – up there, up there – bits of limb all bloody hanging down like decorations.

Ton (*at the window, with urgency*)   Up here, up here!

Kid   I've had enough of you, you pompous git. (*He grabs the* **Head** *by his neck. The* **Head** *whimpers. The* **Kid** *holds the* **Head's** *face above the petrol tank.*) Get away from that window, I ain't pissing now, one false move Farty and he's smoke.

Head   Ah, ah, ah.

Lynne   All right – you've made your point. What do you want us to do?

Kid   That's better.

Lynne   What do you want of us?

Kid   Help me . . . he . . . lp mmmmme. Make a life . . . Help me . . . m . . . m . . . (*His stutter defeats him. Now he is weeping.*) Get a . . . job . . . not factory, not like me brother, all gone grey and old and white . . . and 'at . . . a job . . .

Lynne   If it's a job you want –

Kid   Nice job . . . car and that.

Lynne   We'll help all we can, of course we will.

Kid (*points to the* **Head**)   He's the one gotta help.

Head   I . . . shall.

Kid   'Cause I'm a pupil an' all that.

Head   Yes.

Kid   Anything's possible, you said.

Head   Yes.

Kid   Lying bleeder.

Head   No, no – it is.

Kid   Well then!

Head   Well then, what?

Kid   Promise.

Head   I p . . . p . . . promise, I do.

Kid   Honest.

Head   Aaaaaaah. Fumes . . . choking me.

Lynne   You're choking him, you fool.

Ton   For Christ's sake –

Kid   You gotta promise –

Ton   For God's sake be careful –

Head   I promise!

Kid   Me, a job that –

Head   Yes, yes, YES!

Kid   I want a job . . . a job that – (*He releases the* **Head** *gingerly*.) You said, work hard – everything possible.

Head   If . . . you are prepared to work hard . . .

Kid   Make it possible, make it happen.

Head   Yes . . .

Pause.

Kid   I want . . . to be . . . a brain surgeon.

Pause.

Ton   I'll risk it, I will kill him.

Kid   You said! (*Pause.*) Promise is a promise.

Ton   He's taking the piss in the most devious way –

Head   Did you say, you wished to become –

Kid   I always wanted to be a brain surgeon . . . Doctor Casey . . . Car he had, and bints! Oh, yeah . . . you said here, anything possible.

Ton   I'll take a chance, no one'll know –

Pause. **Ton** *retreats.*

Kid   Well? You promised –

Head   It's not . . . impossible. Not beyond the most remote bounds of . . . possibility. If you work hard.

Ton   Headmaster!

Head   Be quiet.

Lynne   But headmaster.

Head   Silence! Boy here, vocation – a vocation, is it boy?

Kid   Yeah.

Head   Like science, do you?

Kid   Never done it.

Ton   Like offals do you?

Head   Shut up, Mr Peart. Nothing more natural in the world than . . . a boy with spirit, dedication . . . not unintelligent, evening classes, hard work . . . could achieve . . . qualifications. I see no reason why . . . shouldn't . . . give it time . . . patience, hard work . . . oh yes, eventually, medical school . . . become a doctor –

Kid   I said, brain surgeon –

Head   A doctor first –

Kid   I dunno about that.

Head   I think, the best way –

Kid   All right then, I'll take your advice.

Head   Good. Doctor, then specialise.

Kid   On brains.

Head   Quite.

Kid   So, it's possible?

Head   Probable.

Kid   Even though, I never did no exams here, no CSEs or –

Head   Oh, I think qualifications are somewhat overrated, you know –

Kid   Yerr, here – have a fag.

Head   One thinks of Shakespeare . . . Churchill . . . men who achieved, succeeded without the advantage of . . . CSEs.

He laughs, the **Kid** *laughs.* **Ton** *is furious.*

Kid   Churchill eh.

Head   Not a success at school. Nor Milton nor Van Gogh nor –

Kid   Andy Fairweather-Low?

Head   Proves my point. Great shortage of brain surgeons.

Kid   Specially ones without any CSEs.

Head   Always in demand. Excellent career prospects.

Kid   Great.

Head   But, have to work hard.

Kid   Some people'd say – what you're telling me, all a dream. A load of crap to keep me quiet.

Head   Ah –

Kid   But you wouldn't lie to me, would you – wouldn't tell the kids here – the ones who ain't no good at nothing – you wouldn't raise their hopes would you when you didn't mean what you was saying.

Head   Certainly not. Dreams materialise here . . . if you work hard, study hard, apply yourself – application and –

Kid   Be a brain surgeon.

Head   You shall be a brain surgeon if that is what you want.

Kid   And play for West Ham.

Pause.

Striker.

Ton *explodes.*

Ton   Him! He doesn't know a fucking goalpost from an elm tree. He's never done two successive games lessons in his five years here! He can't play football.

Head   Really Mr Peart, you go too far. There are . . . lots of professional footballers who, apparently, lacked ability on the school playing field – to the undiscerning eye . . . I see no reason why what's-'is-name here shouldn't make a first-class professional footballer for West Ham. If he applies himself.

Kid   And be a brain surgeon.

Head   Indeed.

They all nod seriously. The **Kid** *giggles then hysterically.*

Kid   Cunts.

Blackout. Stones' 'Street Fighting Man', loud.

Scene Three

The same night. The Beatles' 'Here Comes the Sun'.

Police cars' blue swirling lights off. The **Head** *and* **Ton** *are asleep on the floor in a corner.* **Lynne** *sits in the centre watching the* **Kid***, who has his shirt wide open, his tie off and is sweating. He is smoking and leaning against the wall beside the bike. A long silence, just the music.*

Kid   All them cops . . . and people . . . and dogs . . . all looking up here. (*Pause.*) I like this song.

Lynne   The Beatles.

Kid   Do you remember The Beatles?

Lynne   God, you make me sound old.

Kid   I heard me brother talk about them. Had their records. Originals, not the re-releases. Funny, in't it. Me mum loves them now. 'Yesterday' and that. When they first come out she used to hate them.

Lynne   Do you think your mum and dad are still down there?

Kid   Dunno. Don't care.

Lynne   Don't you get on with them then?

Kid   Why the fuck did they have to come?

Lynne   Perhaps they . . . just want you to go home with them?

Kid   I ain't going anywhere.

Lynne   What do you think's going to happen when the cigarettes run out?

Kid   We might all be dead by then . . .

Lynne   But you're only sixteen. You don't want to die, do you? I don't want to die yet. How old do you think I am?

Kid   Dunno.

Lynne   Guess.

Kid   Ninety-three.

Lynne   Cheeky sod.

Kid   About twenty-five . . . twenty-six.

Lynne   About that . . . does that sound old to you?

Kid   Not old, is it. Me brother's older than that.

Lynne   The one who delivers leaflets for the Labour Party.

Kid   He did, before he moved.

Lynne   And you've got a gran, who's . . . mad?

Kid   Nar. . . she's dead.

Pause.

Lynne   *Liked* her . . .

Kid   Yeah, I liked her . . . a lot. An' me grandad . . . smart, he was. White silk scarf, tied in a knot . . . old suit . . . but always wore his scarf. . . raced his pigeons . . . put on his suit and tied his scarf and we'd go up to the Fife to deliver the pigeons for the race on a Friday night, you know . . . and Saturday afternoons. . . in the summer. . . waiting in his yard, smoking . . . and talking an' that . . . sun shining . . . waiting . . . for the pigeons to come home. An' one day I said to him, said – 'How do they know where to come back to?' An' he looked at me, an' he said: 'It's the homing instinct . . . in the end, everyone has to come home.'

Pause. He wearily lights another cigarette. New record: from Rod Stewart's Atlantic Crossing, *'This Old Heart of Mine' and 'Sailing'.*

Good bloke he was . . . me grandad . . . no one promised him nothing. No one sold him dreams that weren't gonna happen. So he was happy. With what he got. (*Pause.*) Know what I mean . . . ? (*Pause.*) Oh, this pain . . . in me head. (*Pause.*) Christ. (*He slumps to the floor holding his head.*) Rod Stewart.

Lynne   Yeah.

Kid   Like this, slow side better than the fast side. Never play the fast side. Me brother liked the fast side, but now he's gone, never play it.

Lynne   I prefer this side.

Kid   He took me to see the Faces once . . . at the Rainbow. Queued and queued we did. Got tickets. Went . . . an' it was the night of the bleeding power cuts. No wonder they voted Heath out.

She laughs gently.

Lynne   Good enough reason.

Kid   They akip or what?

Lynne   Exhausted, hungry . . .

Kid   I beat 'em.

Lynne   Yes, you did.

Kid   I ain't tired, ain't hungry.

Lynne   No-o-o . . .

Kid   Funny . . . downstairs . . . they're all still dancing an' outside – cops with cars an' dogs an' that.

Lynne   Life doesn't stop because

Kid   What?

Lynne   Can you dance?

Kid   Leave off. (*He looks out of the window.*) All them, for me.

Silence. He lights another cigarette.

Lynne   You've only got three cigarettes left.

Kid   So?

Lynne   An observation.

Kid   I ain't stupid.

Lynne   No, you're not.

Kid   Ain't clever neither.

Lynne   I'm not sure . . .

Kid   Other people, they get by 'cause they're clever, like Bonny wants 'em to be . . . or good at games like Farty . . . what about . . . me?

Lynne   Other things.

Kid   Yeah, but they don't count.

Lynne   They do.

Kid   How could you go with him?

Lynne   I don't want . . . always to be on my own . . .

Kid   Nar, nor did I . . .

Silence.

What's gonna happen to me . . . what I've done?

Pause.

I said, what's –

Lynne   I don't know . . . don't know, wish I did, could do – I just don't know.

Kid   Shouldn't promise things what you don't mean. That's more wrong than what I done. Achieve, succeed – that pisses me off. But it's what counts, don't it. Trouble is, if you know you ain't achieving, makes it hard. Okay if you dunno.

Lynne   Look. (*Pause.*) What you mustn't do . . . (*Pause.*) Them, don't judge yourself by their standards . . .

*Long silence. Then the **Kid** hits the bike, suddenly turns to her.*

Kid   Dance then?

*They begin to jive. He stops. She strokes his hair; trembling, he begins to cry. She holds him. The **Kid** breaks down. Slowly **Ton** rises and grabs the **Kid** savagely. Holds him down.*

Ton   You bleeder – shit – I'll fucking –

Lynne   Ton, leave him alone – can't you see he's been through enough –

Ton   I'll bloody –

Head   Well done Miss Millar, congratulations. A very clever move.

Lynne   I d . . . didn't mean THAT. It wasn't a trap – (*She screams.*)

Ton *has the **Kid** on the floor.*

Head (*at the window*)   Siege over!

Voices. Blue lights go off. The music stops.

Lynne   I didn't mean – it wasn't meant to . . . get him.

Head   There, there Miss Millar . . . you're overcome . . .
ambulance . . . exhaustion . . . nerves . . . we've all been
through a great ordeal . . . (**Lynne** *looks at* **Ton** *who has the*
Kid *at his feet.*)

Lynne   I didn't mean –

Ton   Okay Lynne, I'll follow you down.

Lynne *hesitates.*

Lynne   I didn't . . . trick you . . . believe me . . . please
. . . it's important that you can . . . believe someone.

The **Kid** *spits in her face. She cries and goes.*

Pause.

Ton *kicks the* **Kid**. *He laughs. The* **Head** *leaves.* **Ton** *kicks the*
Kid *again. The* **Kid** *cries.* **Ton** *kicks savagely. The* **Kid**
whimpers. **Ton** *steps back.*

Blackout. Curtain music: Stones' '19th Nervous Breakdown'.

Getaway

Getaway was first produced on 1 February 1977 at the Soho Poly Theatre Club, London, along with the first two plays of the *Gimme Shelter* trilogy. The cast was as follows:

Kev	Phillip Joseph
Janet	Sharman MacDonald
Gary	Ian Sharp
Kid	Philip Davis

The setting is the boundary of a cricket pitch.

Music

Before the play: hit singles from last summer
After the play: Rolling Stones' 'Gimme Shelter' from the album, *Let It Bleed*

Before lights up, music: hit singles from last summer.

Lights up to reveal a cricket pitch boundary with the sight screen stage right. There are two deckchairs. **Kev** *sits in one wearing cricket whites and pads, reading a newspaper which covers his face.*

Enter **Janet** *eating ice cream: she is discernibly pregnant. The music fades.*

Janet   Bloody liberty. Twenty p a cornet and not even a bit of flakey chocolate on the top. At least for twenty p you'd expect a bit of chocolate on the top. I reckon they saw me coming.

Kev (*still behind his paper*)   Need to be deaf and myopic not to see you coming.

Janet   And the queue! Had to queue up for quarter of an hour. If he'd have sold out – if he'd have sold out I don't know what I'd have done. There'll be no ice cream this afternoon, and then what?

Kev (*putting down the paper*)   You have posed a very intelligent hypothesis. Spain without bullfights – there'd be a revolution. Russia without vodka, they'd occupy the Kremlin. Deny the Chinese rice and rickshaws, the Irish spuds and Guinness, the Israelis circumcision and you have, potentially, a World War Three situation. Deny the bank holiday cricket match with Essex Division ice cream with flakey chocolate and – the entire capitalist world begins to tremble . . .

Janet   I don't know what you're talking about half the time.

Kev   Gary's a selfish bastard. Fifty-six – I'll be bloody lucky to get an innings unless he lashes out a bit.

Janet   I'm right knackered. You'd be surprised how tiring it is walking around with this all day.

Kev   Sit down then Janet. Sit down for gawd's sake – take the weight off your pins.

Janet   Yeah. (*She sits.*) This is putting me right off the idea of one of them Red Indian slings.

Kev   You what?

Janet   Them Red Indian slings. You know, like the squaws carry their kids round in on the reservations. On their back, instead of in a carrycot. It's supposed to be easier. Like you don't feel the weight so much at the back – it's easier to move. You know – like they say Hillman Imps are better 'cause the engine's at the back.

Kev   Definitely.

Janet   Mind you, I'll look nice with a little bundle on me back as I go up the High Street. I'll look like –

Kev   Parachute squad on urban manoeuvres.

Janet   Watch it – I might set Harry on you . . . when he gets here.

Kev   What's up with Harry boy – thought he might have been here today.

Janet   Bank holidays are so good for fares. Especially Jewish bank holidays. He trebles his usual takings.

Kev   Yeah . . . blimey, you do look lovely Jan. I fancy you more than I did last year. If someone last year had told me that twelve months later you'd be married to a taxi driver with a bun in your oven –

Janet   Yeah I know . . . still don't know how it happened. When I threw up after the New Year's Eve party I must have thrown up me birth pill and all.

Kev   The thought of it put me right off potato salad. Give us a bite of that ice cream. You might have got me one.

Janet   Daren't . . . in case it put you off your stroke. Since they told you you were in the team you haven't eaten a proper lunch for . . . days.

Kev   Give us a nibble. (*He goes to her, tickles her, laughs.*)

Janet   Kev – I'm a married lady.

Kev   You still turn me on rotten Janet.

Janet   I'm different now. I'm not like that. A door has closed.

Kev   You might have let me get through it first.

Laughter. Enter the **Kid**. *He is carrying some gardening tools. He watches.* **Janet** *suddenly becomes aware of him and pushes* **Kev** *away. Pause. The* **Kid** *just stands there.*

Janet   You looking for someone, love? (*Pause.*) Are you London office or Essex Division? (*Pause.*) Right chatterbox, ain't you.

Kev   You all right, son?

Kid   Groundsman.

Kev   Oh. It's a lovely pitch. Beautiful wicket. When I saw that wicket I says to Janet here, there's love. And graft. And know-how. Best wicket I've played on all season.

Janet   The only one.

Kev   All right, all right. Mouth. (*To the* **Kid**.) Beautiful pitch.

Kid   Mr Arnold does the wicket, and the pitch. I do the driveway and around the pavilion. The pitch – that's Mr Arnold. He's done it for forty-five years.

Kev   Beautiful, the driveway and around the pavilion and all.

Kid   Oh.

Pause. Applause off.

Kev   What was that?

Janet   Gary – another six!

Kev   Bastard.

Janet   Fantastic!

Kev   Remember what your doctor said – don't over-excite yourself.

Janet   I'll try and keep calm when you're in.

Kev   Yeah. Not mocking. Tail-ender, apart from the openers and the middle-order, the tail-ender can make or break a team. Bondy and Leigh Hunt told me. They said that, when they asked if I was available for selection. They've put a lot of faith in me . . .

Janet   Oh yeah.

Kev   A lot of responsibility . . . bringing up the rear.

Kid   Do you work for them?

Janet   Oh yeah. See, it's the firm's match. Every bank holiday, with Essex Division, every year . . . we always win. We're Holborn. And we always win.

Kev   Always. Curious phenomenon, in a funny way. City Slickers. Hours on the underground . . . cramped living conditions – you'd think this country mob, fresh air, endless pastures, smell of cow-dung in their nostrils – you'd think they'd steamroller us, but we always win. Landslide, last year.

Janet   Last year . . . (*She laughs. Teases* **Kev**.) Remember last year, Kev . . . over there . . .

Kev   A lot can happen in a year.

Kid   I'll drink to that.

Pause.

Janet   Right revolting you was last year . . . eh Kev. Thought you was going to . . . blow 'em up! (*Pause.*) Just sulked instead. (*She touches* **Kev**'s *hair, matily*.)

Kid   Blow 'em up . . . ?

Kev   She's . . . exaggerating.

Janet   Oh yeah? Clive Jenkins? The 'revolution'? But . . . no explosion! Wouldn't be right, would it – for a trainee manager!

Kev   Double luncheon vouchers . . . I conned 'em.

The **Kid** *laughs, surprising them.*

Kid   No . . . blood and bone hanging from the ceiling . . . like Christmas decorations . . . ?

Janet *and* **Kev** *exchange a glance.*

Kid   Funny smell burning flesh . . . hangs in the air for ages . . . *(He kneels and takes his tools out of an ex-army kitbag.)* It's going to be a good autumn for chrysanths . . . soil here is so rich . . . Mr Arnold says the clay below holds it in . . . the goodness . . . nothing is wasted . . .

Kev *is clearly interested in him. He watches the* **Kid** *as he cleans the gardening tools with great care.*

Janet   Such a relief to be able to keep me Polaroids on when you're sunbathing. This pair lets the ultra-violet rays through. Do you remember that year on the beach when you was drunk and you slept all afternoon and me and Gary put your sunglasses on you and when you woke up, where you'd gone red, around your eyes you looked like Coco the Clown?

She laughs, eyes closed behind her glasses. **Kev** *is still studying the* **Kid***.*

Kid   What you looking at?

Kev   Eh?

Kid   Ain't no one told you it's rude to stare?

Kev   What?

Kid   'No one ever told you, boy, it's rude to stare?' Slap. Smash in the face. Didn't mean to hit him with the bike

. . . bang, hit . . . slap . . . pain in me head . . . blew a fuse
. . . Oh. (*His expression switches from defiance to humility. He looks
down and cleans his tools again.*)

Kev *puts a cigarette in his own mouth and offers the packet to the*
Kid.

Kev   Do you smoke?

The **Kid** *grins.*

Kid   No. Not now. Don't smoke. Used to. Not now.

Kev   Better for your health.

Kid   Better for everyone else's health.

'Howzat?' off.

Kev   Hello, hello!

Janet   Kev – Gary's had it!

Kev   Out!

Janet   Just Winston and you're in!

Kev   Oh, I can't wait to get out there. The way that
bloody mob of provincials are bowling – Christ, it'll be like
playing ping-pong with a tennis racket. I hope that sodding
house-magazine photographer hasn't used up all his film.
I'll give him a few spectacular shots. (*He's miming them.*) Sort
of balletic, all-action snaps that'll have the Tate Gallery
begging him to make an exhibition.

Enter **Gary**.

Kev   Unlucky son, unlucky. Know what you did wrong?

Gary   Swung too hard.

Kev   You swung too hard.

Gary   Still, sixty-two ain't bad.

Kev   Oh, it isn't bad. I'll grant you that. In fact, a lot of
people'd say it was very good. I mean, Bondy, put it this

way, Bondy would have been bloody delighted to have got sixty-two. The only thing is . . .

Gary   What?

Kev   Well, it was all – look, you don't mind me giving you an analytical breakdown of where you went wrong, do you?

Gary   Well –

Kev   Frankly, your innings – well, it was distinctly lacking in, how shall I put it? Artistry . . .

Gary   Bullshit.

Kev   Hardly a contribution to the literature of the game. Not a phrase synonymous with John Arlott or to be found idly flicking through the pages of *Wisden*'s – not a word that leaps out at you.

Gary   Artistry, my arse. Sixty-two –

Kev   Good innings, good innings. What I'm saying is – it was all a bit hurried. A bit rushed. No stylised defensive shots, not much off the ol' back foot. No sussing the field and planting nonchalant lobs tantalisingly behind the outlying fielders, you know. The sort of shots that dip just behind cover point and then the bastard has to turn round and give chase to save a four. In vain.

Gary   Kev, I lashed out and got seven sixes.

Kev   That might impress some people –

Gary   Well, blimey. Seven sixes are better than fucking tantalising lobs for four.

Kev   You watch me. I'll show you what I mean. Take me time, a bit of artistry. Oh, what a cool arrogant bastard, they'll say. He's taking his time.

Gary   We need thirty-five from ten overs – got to hurry.

Kev   Ah son, you are confusing speed for hurry. It's like making love and fucking – there's a difference.

Janet   Oh yeah?

Kev   Anyone can fuck. Not many make love. Making love is like serenading on a rare violin. Elephants fuck, you don't get –

Janet   Elephants playing the violin.

Gary   Right! (*He laughs.*) You are a bloody joker, Kev.

Kev   All right, as you like it. They'll be pleased with you tonight Gary. Oh yeah, tonight at the dance, they'll be pretty pleased with you. Of course, the geezer that'll find himself the focus of all the attention'll be the geezer who rattles up the winning run but –

Roars off.

Fuck.

Gary   Winston . . . six.

Kev   Must be bloody contagious. (*He shouts.*) Take it easy boy. Take it easy. (*He sighs.*) There'll be some champagne bubbling tonight, boy. Some corks exploding.

Janet   There's thirty crates. I saw them. Bondy's receptionist told me Bondy had selected them personally himself. He phoned up this chateau in France and got them to fly it all over specially. Bondy has got style –

Kev   I'm surprised Bondy ain't started walking on the fucking water yet.

Gary   He knows about champagne. That do at the Savoy, the wine waiter said Bondy knew more than he did.

Kev   What do at the Savoy?

Gary   For the . . . when the Germans came over.

Kev   You went, did you?

Gary   Yeah.

Kev   I see.

Gary   Six of us from the trainee management course –

Kev   I remember. I was pretty tied up with the Birmingham office then. Sorting out their accounts. Champagne we got through that night. I was cleaning me teeth with it. (*He suddenly becomes again aware of the* **Kid**.) I bet all this sounds terribly bourgeois to you, eh?

Pause.

I know what you're thinking. I thought it at one time. But don't let apparent appearances deceive you. Oh how fucking bourgeois, I expect you're saying to yourself. Am I right, is that what you're saying?

Kid   I dunno what it means . . .

Kev   Ah – you need a political education son.

Gary   From who? (*He laughs.*) Got a beer there Jan – I'm gasping.

Janet   Bit warm, but I kept it covered up with me jumper.

Gary *looks at her.*

Gary   Always keep your jumper on to keep it warm . . .

Pause.

Janet   Yeah well . . . don't have to pay for taxis.

Gary   Right.

Janet   What did she say?

Gary   Eh?

Janet   Clare?

Gary   Oh –

Kev   Clare!

Janet   I'm surprised Bondy brought her, with his wife here.

Kev   What you going on about?

Janet   Well, it's obvious.

Kev   Obvious?

Janet   I mean, if his wife sees just, well, just the way Clare looks at Bondy . . . then she'll know.

Kev   Know? Know what?

Janet   Don't be naive.

Kev   You what?

Janet   Everybody knows.

Kev   If everybody knows, how come I ain't got the foggiest idea what you're going on about.

Janet   Him and her – Clare.

Kev   Bondy and Clare –

Janet   Perhaps they only discuss it at the directors' Christmas parties.

Kev   Oh, that explains it! That's how you speak with such pontifical authority – if it's only discussed at the directors' Christmas parties.

Janet   You know how they used to invite me. Like how now they invite the young girls in typing and that . . . Funny, there being younger girls now. Me talking to the older women, about relaxation classes and that. What did Clare say to you then?

Gary   Well, nothing – she just looked.

Janet   Took long enough.

Kev   Wonder she can bloody see at all with all that crap round her eyes. Looks like she's been peering through a pair of binoculars with the lenses smothered in black emulsion paint.

Janet   What if she makes a pass at you at the dance tonight?

Gary   Leave off!

Janet   Just to get at Bondy – for bringing his wife.

Kev   Eh?

Janet   Oh, don't be so naive, Kev. Everyone knows how he takes Clare on all his trips . . . Munich and Amsterdam and Paris and the conferences at Blackpool.

Kev   How very cosmopolitan. There is nothing more disgusting than bourgeois gossip –

Kid   What?

Pause.

Kev   Bourgeois . . . (*Pause.*) French. (*Pause.*) Middle class. Wider connotations, in a political focus as it were . . . synonymous with – *the enemy.*

Longer pause.

Kid   Whose enemy?

Kev   Exactly!

Janet   Winston's arf put on weight.

Gary   Eh?

Janet   Last year he looked so slim . . . and now look at him.

Kev   All them bloody accountants' lunches. To be an accountant, you need a strong stomach more than a head for figures.

Gary   You want a beer, mate?

Kid   Oh . . . I can't take it.

Gary   Course you can.

Kid   For me?

Gary   Yeah.

Kid   Mr Arnold drinks half a bottle of whisky a day.
Sometimes the boundary line has a bend in it. He says he's
looping the loop. (*He laughs. The others don't.*)

(*Pause.*) All right, ta. (*He opens the can. Cuts his finger.*) Shit!
Bloody tin.

Janet   It's bleeding –

Gary   Blimey, you bleed easily.

Janet   Let it bleed, that's the best thing. Clears out any
germs – just let it bleed.

The **Kid** *holds up a dripping, bloody finger and stares at it with
fascination.*

Janet   Put it away, do me a favour – it's making me
stomach turn.

Kid   There was a bloke . . .

Pause.

In Feltham . . . he got a razorblade . . . they took them
away but he saved them up . . . he took the mattress off his
bed, and where there was the wooden frame, he made slits,
and stuck the razor blades in them . . . they all stood up . . .
some was broken. He ran into the door, with his head . . .
metal door, like cells are . . . and when he was really dizzy,
he threw himself on the bed and the blades went in here
and here and here and here . . . and one went in his throat.
I emptied his shit bucket and filled it with water and
washed up the blood . . . and I never saw him again.

Silence.

Janet   I'm going to get some ice creams, would anyone
like one?

They ignore her and she goes.

Gary   Feltham?

Kid   Nine months.

Gary   What is it?

Kid   Ain't Butlin's.

Kev   It's a kinda Borstal . . . in't it?

Kid   For loons. (*He giggles, pause.*) I ain't a loon.

Gary   What did you do?

Kid   Nothin'.

Gary   Then why –

Kid   What I nearly did.

Gary   What?

Kid   B . . . b . . . blow 'em up!

Gary   Who?

Kid   Me school. Last day . . . they was shitting themselves. Got this . . . pain in me head. I didn't know what I was doing. Didn't mean it. At Feltham, this trick cyclist . . . he said at least it would have been better if I'd meant it. He said then he'd have understood.

Kev   You tried to . . . blow up your school?

Kid   Leave off, not the whole school. I ain't no Guy Fawkes. Just some of the people in it . . . with me motorbike . . . didn't do it . . .

Pause.

Kev   In Rainham.

Kid   Yeah.

Kev   I read about it. In the papers. It was you. It was you!

Kid   They didn't say who it was. They weren't allowed to use me name – 'cause I'm a juvenile.

Kev   All that, and they don't even use your name. Anonymous. That's a bastard.

Kid   Nar.

Kev   Oh Christ, Oh Christ! Don't you remember, Gary? Christ, the publicity! Papers full of it. Afterwards, *Panorama* did a whole programme – 'The Twilight World of Educational No-Hopers.' Robin Day got his glasses steamed up with Roy Hattersley and –

Kid   I must've missed that.

Kev   Even Maggie Thatcher got in on the act. Said this was exactly what you expected when inflation ran at 16 per cent.

Kid   I didn't know what none of them was on about.

Kev   And no one said it was you. No name. Never.

Kid   Glad about that. Me mum had to go on tranquillisers and her hair went white. (*Pause.*) Here, I'm not allowed to talk about it. When Mr Arnold took me on it was on the strict understanding that no one knew about it. If anyone knows, I'll be out on me arse.

Kev   You can rely on me.

Kid   Hard getting a job after Borstal. This place here, they're very good. They take you on. I'm going.

The **Kid** *attempts to go.* **Kev** *holds him.*

Kev   Hang about, hang about. I want to shake you by the hand.

Kid   What?

Kev   I want to shake you by the hand.

Kid   Eh?

Kev   Your hand.

Kid   It's still bleeding.

Kev   Scars of the revolution. Like me.

Kid   Eh?

Kev   Daren't take me shirt off when I'm sunbathing. Less the scars of the class struggle on me back show. Frighten the horses.

Gary   Clare's fingernails.

Kev   Sit down son, sit down. (*He forces the* **Kid** *into a chair.*)

Kid   Nar, gotta go, gotta getaway.

Kev   An' old colonels kept writing letters to *The Times.* 'Is this what is meant by Socialist comprehensive education?' Like it was all part of the liberal studies curriculum, or something.

Kid   Look, I don't wanna talk about it. It's over. Something that happened. I've served me time, repaid me debt to society and all that, right. I've started again. School, waste of bleeding time. Feltham though, showed me how to . . . give me a trade. Fantastic job. Out all weathers. All summer, out in the open. I was in charge of the vegetable gardens. Growed things, and ate 'em. Learned a lot. Got it made now. When I left, the governor, he said to me: 'You've achieved two things. Learned a trade. Gardener. And you've found respect in yourself.' (*Slight pause.*) I've got respect in meself now.

Kev   For Christ's sake. You had more respect in your little toenail the day you –

Kid (*leaps out of the chair*)   Shut up! Don't talk about it!

Kev   For Christ's sake, why not?

Kid   'Cause I wanna forget about it, right! In the past, don't wanna keep looking back. Mistake. Made a mistake.

Now, forget it, look forward to stuff. Got respect, ain't I? Make a go of things. Not keep raking up last year.

Kev (*forcing the* **Kid** *back into the chair. Impassioned*)   That's what I'm saying. That's why I want to shake your hand, son. 'Cause it was . . . a start. It . . . thrilled me.

Kid   I dunno what you're talking about.

Kev   For Christ's sake! Can't you see it? It thrilled hundreds, it thrilled thousands, what you did. It gave hope. Your great gesture, a spark of the inevitable . . . revolution. It should be blazed across England.

Gary   Leave him alone, Kev.

Kid   He don't understand.

Kev   But I *do* understand. I do. You did, you did what I wanted to do. You did it.

Kid   Bollocks.

Kev (*holding the* **Kid** *in the chair, almost pleading*)   I'm serious. Felt your anger. Your rage. You took the great leap and let it go.

Kid   I didn't let it go, thank Christ I didn't let it go.

Kev   I wish you had done.

Kid   You're mad. (*To* **Gary**.) He's mad, in't he?

Kev   Wish it had gone further. The supreme gesture.

Kid   Look, I'm all straight now, so don't you start messing me up.

Kev   I'm not messing you up. It's them, over there, them up there, them who dash up and down compromising, keeping the status quo in balance, they're the ones who're the ones who're messing you up. What you did . . . you was right.

Kid   Stop trying to . . . mix me up. I've got it together now.

Kev   You gave hope. You breathed life into the dream
that . . . things, this England . . . 1976 . . . can be changed.

Kid   I've changed.

Kev   For the worse.

Kid   Don't you fucking tell me. I'm not getting mixed up
again. I'm happy now.

Kev   What, watering the dahlias?

Kid   You're mad.

Kev   What if when Lenin got the call in Zurich, what if
he'd said – 'Sorry mate, I've got to weed me window-box'?

Kid   I dunno what you're talking about.

Kev   Jesus, kid – what I'm saying is, thank you, for that
inspiration. We all know everything's wrong. But there's
gotta be a moment when it can all . . . happen. Your
moment showed it ain't a dream.

Kid   A dream? I fucking dreamed about it, in Feltham.
Fucking nightmare. That I dropped the fag, the petrol
went and the bodies burned. The eyes popped. The bellies
exploded. Burned flesh, like sticky black plastic, stuck to
me face, closed me eyes, I couldn't see.

Kev   Yeah, well – what I'm saying is: Your anger, your
rage . . . I know that rage. Could have been me in that
room. Got to unify angers. Not waste it. Together we –

Kid   We?

Silence.

Shake me by the hand, you say. Might get yours dirty.

Kev   We're on the same side. We are. Look on me as
. . . like the Red Cross. Behind the lines. Patching up
the warriors. Sending them back over the top. Fifth
column. Infiltrating. Ready to use the knowledge I've
absorbed –

Gary   Kev!

Kev   What?

Gary   Kev, you've changed sides.

Kev   Haven't, haven't! Just . . . look like it. See you kid, I see myself. See I was right.

Pause.

Kid *(stands up, derisive)*   I'll leave it to you then. (*He picks up the tools.*) You make me laugh. (*He begins to go, turns, laughs.*) Ain't had such a good laugh for ages.

The **Kid** *has gone. Pause.* **Kev** *shouts after him.*

Kev   You can't walk away from your rage. You can't walk away from it. Day'll come they'll chant your name. Whatever it is.

Gary   Winston, only need two to win.

Kev   Dunno what . . . just know I gotta . . . (*He sits wearily.*) I might as well take off the pads . . .

Pause.

Gary   You never know, way he's slogging, you could go in . . . Only need two to win.

Kev   I'll take off the pads. (*He begins to take off the pads.*)

Gary   Moving in the fielders . . . tricky end and all . . . from the sea-front . . . rubbing the ball.

Enter **Janet**.

Janet   You'll never guess – Pia's here and guess what, she's going to have twins!

Gary   Hang on Janet . . . look –

Janet   What?

Gary   Winston . . . only need two runs to win.

Janet   Oh yeah . . . Pia's having twins, did you hear
Kev? Pia, she's so happy . . . and the mortgage has come
through, this lovely place at Hornchurch, a bit too
expensive, she said, but they've got the mortgage over
thirty years so they can afford it . . . and they'll all be
moved in, out of that rotten flat and have the house
decorated and ready in time for the birth, oh how
smashing. See, I told her not to give up hope, when they
was living with his in-laws, and however terrible it seemed
then, I knew it'd work out for the best.

Gary   And here it comes . . .

The light begins to fade. **Kev** *sits, head in hands, slumped in his
deckchair.* **Janet** *and* **Gary** *both look at the pitch expectantly.
Applause.*

Gary   We've won. (*He looks at* **Kev**.) Again . . .

*A very slow fade. Fade in Rolling Stones' 'Gimme Shelter'. The three
characters freeze as light fades slowly to blackout and volume of music
increases.*

Barbarians

Killing Time
Abide With Me
In the City

Barbarians was first produced as a trilogy at the Greenwich Theatre, London, on 29 September 1977, with the following cast:

Paul	Nick Edmett
Jan	Karl Johnson
Louis	Jeffery Kissoon

Directed by Keith Hack
Designed by Voytek

The following music was used for the Greenwich production:

Before *Killing Time*: The Clash's 'Career Opportunities'
After *Killing Time*: Sex Pistols' 'Anarchy in the UK'
Before *Abide With Me*: Sex Pistols' 'Pretty Vacant'
After *Abide With Me*: The Clash's 'Police and Thieves'
Before *In the City*: The Jam's 'In the City'
Curtain Music: Sex Pistols' 'God Save the Queen'

The setting throughout was a brick and corrugated iron wall covered with graffiti.

Killing Time

A play in one act

Killing Time was first produced by the National Youth Theatre at the Soho Poly Theatre Club, London, on 22 August 1977 with the following cast:

Paul	Michael Kelly
Jan	Robert Glenister
Louis	Dotun Adebayo

(Shane Anderson played Misog and Ashley Burns the chauffeur; these two characters were cut for the Greenwich production and have been cut from this text.)

Directed by Bill Buffery

Lights up on an empty stage: the back wall smothered with ripped posters and graffiti. Old bits of newspapers on the floor, discarded cigarette boxes and coke cans.

Jan, *sixteen, doing a handstand against the back wall.*

Music fades.

Jan   Life is a shit sandwich. The more bread you've got, the less shit you have to swallow.

Pause. **Paul**, *all nervous energy, older, comes on. He sees* **Jan**, *hesitates, then runs at him and kicks away* **Jan**'s *hands.* **Jan** *falls.*

Jan   Whatcher do that for?

Paul   I felt like it.

Jan   Just minding me own business standing upside down . . .

Paul   You look more of a prick on your feet than your head.

Jan   England makes more sense upside down.

Paul   How did it go?

Jan   Oh, it was another wank.

Paul   I told you not to go. Why humiliate yourself?

Jan   Gotta go, ain't I.

Paul   To be humiliated?

Jan   Guess who I saw there?

Paul   Half the class from last year.

Jan   Apart from them . . . outside the job centre, guess who I saw?

Paul   Fucking Prime Minister.

Jan   The careers officer, from school – remember him?

Paul   The bloke who kept pissing his trousers?

Jan   Yeah him.

Paul   At the job centre?

Jan   An', see, I see him and I twigged it, didn't I? He's on the fucking dole, in't he? They give him the elbow. Now he's on the fucking dole.

Paul   Loverly. They offer you anything?

Jan   Tin Box factory.

Paul   You tell him what to do with it?

Jan   I said, 'I ain't having that. It's all fucking bints, in't it.' He says: 'You bent?' I says, 'I ain't fucking doing a bint's job.' I said: 'Choosy, ain't I.'

Paul   Should have shot the bastard.

Jan   Yeah.

Paul   There's another forty thousand leaving next week. An' still they ain't got nothing for all us who left last year!

Jan   Deaths.

Paul   What?

Jan   A lot died, in the year.

Paul   Yeah.

Jan   If forty thousand died every year –

Paul   Yeah?

Jan   Be all right, wouldn't it?

Paul *sniffs, paces.*

Paul   When you get killed in a car smash, you come. Cousin told me.

Jan   How's he know?

Paul   Breaker's yard, got a job in a breaker's yard.

Jan   Get you in?

Paul   Nar, it's gone broke. He said: car smashes, write-offs, they're full of spunk. You shoot it all over the windscreen.

Jan   I don't believe it.

Paul   He found a penis in a writ-off Cortina. The ambulance man must have forgot to put it in his little plastic bag. Me cousin said it had lipstick marks round the top.

Jan   Wow.

Paul   Geezer went through the winder, head first.

Jan   What a way to go! I never knew that. I wouldn't mind a breaker's yard.

Paul   Me cousin would have had me like a shot. At the yard. But he went down.

Jan   I know.

Paul   When he come out, the geezer he'd left in charge, this geezer had sold off all the gear and legged it. To Canada. To be a Mounty. Me cousin was all for getting off after him. Things he was going to do to him. He was gonna hatchet him. Chop off his prick with a pair of rose pruners. Me old man talked him out of it.

Jan   Good.

Paul   He said, 'Come off it Keith. It just ain't on. I mean, it just ain't on. You piss off to Canada and chop the prick off a fucking Mounty.'

Jan   Right.

Paul   You kidding?

Jan   What?

Paul   Really, the careers officer?

Jan   He told me. I said, 'What you doing here then?' He said, 'I'm on the fucking dole same as you.'

Paul   That's rich. Me mum's going up the wall.

Jan   Taken a photo?

Paul   She's up the spout again . . .

Jan   Does your dad know?

Paul   He said he did it.

Jan   Did he?

Paul   How the fuck should I know. Think he must've. He hit her when she told him.

Jan   Cunt.

Paul   Not hard. Still . . . not the thing to do is it. It ain't exactly love story at the flicks. 'Dwarling, we're gonna have a baby.' Wallop round the head. I mean, that ain't exactly – not Hollywood.

Jan   Nar, nor's a lot of other things. You've got to get out. Get a room.

Paul   Gonna get a flat ain't we!

Jan   You ain't mentioned it.

Paul   Well, need the old bread first right. As soon as one of us gets a fucking job . . . right . . . get a flat.

Jan   Oh good. What's tonight then?

Paul   Car-spotting, in't it.

Jan   What's he want now?

Paul   Wants a Rover 3,500.

Jan   Eh?

Paul   You heard. Ideally like – left-hand drive.

Jan   There's no Rover 3,500s round here. Fucking left-hand drive!

Paul   French order.

Jan   Fuck that. I mean, left-hand drive Rover 3,500s ain't exactly thick on the ground in Lewisham, are they?

Paul   Try up town. Newer the better.

Jan   Tonight?

Paul   Phone him soon as we see one . . . he's got the geezers standing by. Hyst it tomorrer and strip it in twenty-four hours. Be in France Saturday.

Jan   Left-hand drive though.

Paul   That's ideal. Don't matter. Come on, few quid. Something to do anyway . . . only otherwise killing time ain't we?

Jan   Right. How we get up West End then?

Paul   Louis, he'll have some bread . . . for the fares.

Jan   Yeah.

Paul   Sister leaves him a quid under the mat outside the door. Leaves the light in the hall on.

Jan   I'd poke her, I ain't fussy.

Paul   He'll just be pissing around somewhere. If she's got a geezer in. And he'll have a quid . . .

Jan   There he is, wanking again.

Lights off and suddenly up on **Louis** *who speaks directly at someone in the first row of the audience. He holds* Whitehouse *magazine.*

Louis   One night the bleeding bulb had gone, hadn't it. In the hall. I gets back, no light on, so I goes in don't I and there she is with her skirt up round her waist on the mat in front of the telly and this great white hairy arse pumping up and down on top of her. I'll give 'em their dues, they didn't get it out like. Nar, she just starts having a go at me don't she. She says, 'What the fuck you doing in here?' I said, I says: 'I come in for me tea, ain't I.' She says, 'Get out willya.' Still this great hairy white arse up and down,

up and down. He don't even look at me, does he. I says,
'That's nice in't it. I got more rights to come in here and
have me tea than you have to be doing that.' I mean,
there's a time and place for everything ain't there. And
Match of the Day's on the telly, Millwall. Jimmy Hill doing a
slow-motion replay bit how this bloke got it from the
narrowest of angles and I thought: You're fucking telling
me! I was a bit pissed 'cause I'd had this bit of luck with a
parking meter like and I'd had this half bottle of Johnny
Walker see and just sits there and the guy goes Errrrrr.
Flakes out, looks up, hadn't even noticed I'd come in.
Looks round, it's the fucking geography teacher ain't it! He
says, 'You cunt.' I says, 'That's nice – in me own home,
like.' This is when I was at school, weren't it. Next day,
makes me do five-mile cross country, don't he! Says I'm
athletic don't he. Fed up people saying I'm athletic.
Anyone tells me I'm athletic – I know they're trying to con
me. He says I could be an Olympic sprinter. Be a British
hero he says, in the Moscow Olympics. Yeah, British hero
in Moscow. In Lewisham I'd still be a bloody nigger.

Looks at magazine.

Louis   I wonder if it's the *same Whitehouse?*

Now **Jan** *and* **Paul** *are either side of him.* **Paul** *snatches the*
magazine.

Paul   All this wanking Louis son.

Louis   I weren't wanking.

Paul (*quietly*)   Too much wanking makes your ears go
funny.

Louis   Pardon?

Paul (*shouts*)   I said: Too much wanking makes your ears
go funny.

Louis   Oh.

Jan   Does your sister fancy me?

Louis   Nar, you're on the bleeding dole. She only likes boys with money.

Paul   Teachers!

Louis   History teacher last night. This rate she'll go through the whole staffroom and when I was there I never been inside it.

Jan   Saw the careers teacher on the dole.

Louis   On the dole!

Paul   He's on the dole, they give him the elbow.

Louis   Serves him right. He never knew what he was talking about. He was the one who –

Jan   I know, I know.

Louis   He said, go on this government training course.

Paul   He told everyone that. You was the only stupid prat who believed him.

Louis   Refrigeration, he said train in that. He said everything'll be frozen soon. He said it's the coming thing. He said go on the training course, they guarantee you a job if you do the year's training. Did the whole bloody year. I'm an expert in refrigeration.

Jan   Yeah, all that.

Louis   I could freeze anything. If I had something to freeze. If I had the equipment and the tools, I could turn me hand at any sort of refrigeration job. Pity there ain't none.

Paul   You got the quid then?

Louis   Nar not tonight, she ain't got no one up there tonight.

Jan   What's up with her?

Louis   Me mum's home ain't she.

Paul   Lost her job?

Louis   Nar, no cleaning tonight . . . they got a do up there ain't they. Banquet, ain't it.

Jan   You what?

Louis   There's this do up there – so the cleaners did it this afternoon. Mum arf nicked a lot of fags – here have one.

They all light cigarettes.

What the thing is . . . look.

Paul (*reads brochure*)   'The Mayor's Banquet will be served with a variety of European wines and as in other similar banquets the loyal toast is to be drunk in the words of Dickens with all due enthusiasm . . . smoking before the loyal toast is considered a serious breach of et . . . eti . . . eti . . . quat. And this rule is never relaxed although on rare occasions the loyal toast has been proposed earlier than usual to suit the comfort of a very distinguished guest, such on one notable occasion President Eisenhower . . . Tonight's guest of honour will be Mr R.W. Kershaw, the Borough's Youth Employment Officer.

Jan   With musical entertainment by Bob Marley.

Louis   You're joking – honest?

Paul   Fuck off.

Louis   She's going up there early in the morning . . . after they have banquets up there, the fucking food they chuck away.

Paul   Counting on fare from you to get up town for a motor.

Louis   I'm fed up spotting motors for your cousin. Costs more spotting them than he pays us for phoning him.

Jan   You got a better idea?

Pause.

Louis   What motor?

Jan   He wants a left-hand drive Rover 3,500.

Louis   Left-hand drive – I've never seen a left-hand drive, not a Rover 3,500. Not in Lewisham.

Paul   That's why we wanna go up West in'it. Hotels.

Louis   What's he want a left-hand drive for anyway?

Paul   Frenchman.

Jan   They drive left-handed on the Continent.

Louis   Bloody mad. One of Sylvie's boyfriends was gonna go to Spain in his motor, weren't he. And Sylvie's other geezer says they drive on the other side of the road over there. So's next week he comes round and Sylvie was thinking he might take her with him to Spain and he says, 'Nar, I ain't going. This driving on the other side of the road lark. I tried it on the South Circular last night and it's fucking murder.'

Paul   Daft spade.

Louis   He weren't a spade, she never goes with spades . . . she hates black blokes, she says they've never got no money.

Jan   Don't matter if it ain't left-handed. That was preference.

Paul   Tell you what . . . lot of motors outside Tiffany's. Have a butchers at Tiffany's like?

Jan   Come on . . .

Louis   All right, I'll come with you then.

Jan   His mum's up the spout again.

Louis   Again, blimey! Must be something they put in the water at your flats.

Paul   That's all I need. Another fucking brother.

Jan   Let's take a butchers at the motors at Tiff's.

Jan *and* **Louis** *retreat and* **Paul** *addresses the audience.*

Paul   I think he did it deliberate, like giving her another
one to tie her down. They was cutting back and they
stuffed him on the night shift, like. On the night shift at his
age. He didn't fancy it, but they was cutting back, see.
Thought he'd keep her out of mischief so give her another
one. Gonna seem funny, calling a bleeding baby a brother.
He tried to get me in there, but they was cutting back. It's
all been a waste of bleeding time since . . . I can't
remember when it weren't a waste of bleeding time.
School was a waste of bleeding time. Everything was
boring. This careers bloke kept rubbing it in, he kept
saying he did, future is in your hands, he said. Yeah, yeah
. . . like trying to catch a fucking Frisby in the wind. He
was right panicked all the time. Tell you the truth, I felt
sorry for the bloke, I did. Dashing about trying to fit
people up and he knew, and we knew and *he knew we knew*
that it was all fucking hopeless, but it's hard to imagine. He
said once, he said . . . look here, he said, imagine
Wembley, Cup Final . . . all them people, hundred
thousands he said. Right, imagine that. He said that's how
many school-leavers have been on the dole for more than a
year. So he says, you've got to make yourself presentable
ain't you, make yourself presentable, get in there, get stuck
in. Tell yourself you ain't gonna be one of them. So's what
did I do, I bought a suit didn't I. Fucking suit. For the
interviews. Traipsing round all keen at first, so's I wouldn't
be one of them and . . . I give it to me brother when he got
married. Eight quid seventy, a week. I was better off when
I did the milk round when I was at school. I was buying
records then, I bought an album most weeks. Spot the
motor for me cousin, be a few quid . . . no trouble, at
Tiffany's.

Flashing coloured lights downstage and music: Status Quo. Loud at

*first then fading down so we can hear them speak. They face the
audience in a straight line; the audience is the foyer of Tiffany's. Just*
Jan *and* **Louis**.

Jan   All in their lovely clothes.

Louis   At least rocker girls show a bit of leg.

Jan   Yeah.

Louis   They wear stockings. At least with rocker girls,
you can see up their fucking skirts.

Jan   Stupid-looking Teds. And their bints look fantastic.

Louis   Me sister had a Ted once.

Jan   What, Sylvie had a Ted?

Louis   Yeah, she says you gotta try things when you get
the chance. She said it took him about a half an hour to
get his bleeding drainpipes off.

Jan   We're never gonna find a left-hand drive Rover
round here.

Louis   Now if it was a left-hand drive Cortina . . .

Pause.

Jan   What?

Louis   I never seen a left-hand drive Cortina in
Lewisham neither.

Jan   Have to go up West for the Rover, have to be right-
hand drive.

Louis   Well, right-hand drive Rover – there's hundreds.
That's no problem. See I've been thinking it had to be left-
hand drive that's why I weren't really looking. Never get a
left-hand drive –

Jan   You say everything three times.

Louis   Eh?

Jan   You say the same thing three times.

Louis   Yeah, well boy – I gotta lot of time on me hands. Dead cinch finding a right-hand drive Rover.

Paul *comes on.*

Paul   Not a fucking Rover in the car park, not a Rover in sight.

Louis   I was just saying –

Paul   What?

Louis   You ain't gonna get a left-hand drive Rover, not here.

Paul   Go up West, the hotels. Good chance there. I mean, he said right-hand'll be all right.

Louis   Oh well, that'll be all right.

Paul   Anything. Bloody waiting list. Pay a grand over the top for a new Rover 3,500. There's a lot of fucking money about.

Louis   Yeah, you should see the things me mum's been bringing home from the charring – bloody leg of ham.

Jan   She'll get done sooner or later.

Louis   Nar, it's all right. They put her in charge of security ain't they. She has to look in the other women's bags don't she . . . that's when she does the nicking. Her and the security guard bloke. Leg of ham size of . . . size of . . . for this banquet. The Mayor's Banquet.

Paul   Ain't seen you flashing it.

Louis   Yeah, well . . . went off in the heat didn't it. I could have refrigerated it, could have . . . if I'd had the equipment and a fucking refrigerator. I could freeze anything, given the equipment and a refrigerator I'm an expert, mate. When I left the training course, the teacher he says: 'You're an expert in refrigeration.' I was right chuffed, first time I've ever been called an expert. He said: 'Refrigeration is the same in any language.' Think someone would have wanted a refrigeration expert. Bloody funny that. A whole year –

Paul   He fucking goes on.

Louis   Yeah, boy – watch it. You're talking to a refrigeration expert.

Paul   One kick with the right boots and this whole winder'd go in.

Jan   And the bouncer'd strangle you.

Paul   Nasty bastards. No Rovers in the car park. Have to go up West . . .

Jan   Yeah. Got any money though?

Paul   Forty p.

Louis   Forty p, that all you got?

Paul   How much you got?

Louis   Oh . . . yeah well . . . I got thirty-five.

Jan   I wouldn't mind going in there . . . hang about, have a couple of pints, you know.

Louis   Yeah.

Paul   I had a shifty. Fire exit's locked, in't it. Stupid thing to lock a fire exit. Supposed to be open so you can get out in a fire.

Louis   What about –

Paul   What?

Louis   What about, we set a fire in there and then they'll open the fire exit and we can get in?

Paul   You prat.

Jan   What's the point of going in if it's on fire?

Pause.

Louis   Oh yeah.

Paul *talks directly to a girl in the front row of the audience.*

Paul   You fancy me, don't you?

Jan   She's looking at you.

Paul   Whatcher!

Louis   She's looking away. Leave off, you're embarrassing her.

Paul   Don't blush, if you played your cards right you could have me.

Jan   Wouldn't play snap to have you.

Paul   I'm all yours. If you can lend me the money to get in. Ain't got-no-money so they won't let me in. (*Pulls out pockets to show and coins drop.*)

Louis *smiles at the girl, strikes a moody pose. Cigarette dangling from lips.*

Paul   Fucking James Dean of Lewisham. Ain't it never occurred to you . . . you can't be James Dean. He was white.

Louis   That was on the outside. Oh Christ, I wanna see them movies again. When they're on somewhere. I wouldn't mind getting killed in a car crash. If I had a car, what a way to go.

Jan   Rebel without a car.

Louis   Before I get a car though . . . get a leather jacket like, and this white T-shirt like, and some winkle-picker cowboy boots like and come up here, won't I –

Jan   When's this?

Louis   Oh, when I gotta job and got some money, like. I'll come up here, lean on the bar, you know, in the corner, hunch me shoulders up like, squint a bit like – see, he was short-sighted – so I'll hunch me shoulders and lean against the corner of the bar dead moody and rebellious like, right mysterious like, and they'll all think: Who's that dark mystery man who looks just like James Dean?

Paul   Have the car smash after?

Louis   Well, not if I've pulled anyone. Wouldn't like to smash up me Porsche if I've got this bint in it with me who's mad about me, you know.

Jan   That's very decent of you.

Louis   Wouldn't want to kill her and all. I wonder if you know when you're dead? I wonder if the dead know they're dead?

Jan   I'll ask 'em at the factory.

Paul   The factory?

Jan   If I went, I mean.

Paul   Bint's job – that ain't a job for a geezer, in a factory with bints.

Louis   They trying to get you to go there – the factory with the bints?

Jan   Don't miss a fucking thing do you?

Louis   I turned that down. Not gonna do a girl's job am I?

Paul   No way, that's right. Not a girl's job.

Jan   Nar . . . but, did think . . . just to fill in a few weeks like, something to do, bit of proper money.

Paul   No way, it's not on.

Jan   Nar.

Louis   Tell them what to do with it.

Jan   Yeah, I did.

Paul   What did he say?

Pause.

Jan   He said . . . 'Fussy, ain't you.'

Paul   You stay fussy. Stick to your entitlements.

Jan   Right.

Louis   Stick to your entitlements, that's what I say.

Paul   You bet.

Louis   Just see meself in a factory with bints. I'm an expert in refrigeration. Done the year's training.

Jan   I ain't.

Louis   Shows I weren't a prune then, don't it.

Paul   I got it. I got it. Tell you where there's a good chance there'll be a bloody Rover 3,500 – why didn't I think of it before. You know where they all go with their flash cars, to screw, on the flats, by the duck pond . . . fucking in the open on the flats.

Jan   Right.

Paul   Go and spot the motor there, give me cousin a buzz – tenner each in.

Louis   Right.

Jan   Good thinking, Batman.

Paul   That's where me cousin took his bints before he got his own place. In the motor. Have it off by the duck pond. Straight out of the Young Tories . . .

Jan   Eh?

Paul   Used to go to the Young Tories' dances, didn't he. Said Young Tory bints, fuck like rattlesnakes, don't they. If you've got the readies. Go like rattlesnakes.

Louis   I wonder if Margaret Thatcher was a Young

Tory . . . when she was young?

Louis and **Paul** *exit, laughing.*

Jan (*to audience*)   His cousin's got it all sussed out . . . since he's been out. Great bloke, his cousin. Really smart . . . they're really close. Gonna have Paul in his business with him, when Paul gets his licence. He can supply anything . . . Tell him the motor you want, he'll get it for you. Like waiting list for new Jags – there's no waiting list with his cousin. Rovers, great! Every new model, he's laughing. Every strike, he's over the moon. He bungs us thirty quid for spotting the one he's after . . . If they can afford the motors, serves the bastards right when they have 'em nicked. That's what his cousin says. Must be nice, to have a cousin like that . . .

The three leaning against the back wall; half light.

Jan   E-Type . . .

Louis   Audi, Audi   lot of Audis about.

Paul   And . . . would you believe . . . Rover 3,500.

Louis   No way that's gonna be left-hand drive.

Paul   I tell you, that was only ideal.

Jan   Fantastic.

Paul   Yeah, but how long's he gonna be there?

Jan   Half an hour . . .

Louis   Depends, don't it.

Paul   No good.

Jan   Latest registration – dead right.

Paul   How's he gonna nick it if the geezer's sitting in it, you clown?

Jan   Oh yeah.

Paul   Parked car! Stupid idea, coming here.

Louis   Could have been up West by now.

Jan   Wait a minute, wait a minute . . . they're getting out.

Louis   Hot night, in't it.

Paul   Fucking in the open, disgusting, pervert.

Louis (*shouts*)   Perverts.

Paul (*clasps hand over* **Louis***'s mouth*)   Shut up, idiot.

Jan   Idiot.

Pause.

Paul   So's what we do . . . make it right easy, extra
tenner . . . what we do . . . when he drops his pants, right . . .
finger the keys outa the pocket, right. They'll have to go
home on the bleeding bus – ring me cousin, hand him the
keys when he gets here to drive it off. Well, what d'yer say?

Pause.

Okay then Louis?

Louis   Ah, come off it . . . I ain't going over there and
picking his pocket while the geezer's on the job. What you
take me for?

Jan   You're used to it – be just like home.

Louis   Leave off . . . it's one thing phoning up your
cousin telling him we've spotted a motor. It's another thing
nicking keys in't it.

Pause.

In't it?

Paul   Chicken.

Louis   I ain't chicken.

Jan   Well, do it then.

Pause.

Louis   Why me? It's your cousin.

Paul   I gotta phone him, ain't I.

Louis   I'll phone him.

Paul   You don't know the number.

Louis   Tell me then.

Paul   My contact, in't it.

Louis (*to* **Jan**)   You do it then.

Jan   You're more athletic than me.

Louis   Every time something blows out, someone tells me I'm athletic. I ain't athletic.

Jan   It's getting dark, he'll never see you coming.

Louis   Course he'll see me coming.

Paul   Not if you lay on the floor . . . wriggle along, you know, like a snake and that . . .

Louis   And pick the bloke's pocket?

Paul   Right.

Louis   While his trousers are round his ankles?

Jan   That's it.

Louis   On top of the bird?

Paul⎫
        ⎬   Yeah!!!
Jan ⎭

Pause.

Louis   I got me best trousers on.

Paul   So what?

Louis   I might get dog shit on them.

Paul   Extra tenner, be worth it.

Louis Say he sees me . . . he'll think I'm a bleeding pervert meself.

Jan Hammer him.

Louis Suppose he shouts help?

Paul I'll be right behind you, kick him one, and we're off.

Louis Bloke on the job, turns round and sees my face and my hand going down his pockets . . .

Paul *begins to walk away.*

Paul That's it, finished with you. Come on Jan.

Jan Yeah, he's chicken.

Paul Just see James Dean chickening out of –

Louis You leave Jimmy out of this!

Paul He'd do it like no one's business.

Louis I know he would.

Paul Well then!

Louis Hmmmm. (*Scratches his head.*) All right then. I'll do it. But the extra tenner's mine then?

Jan Okay.

Paul Yeah, it's a deal.

Louis And you promise not to tell no one?

Paul No way.

Louis 'Cause it's criminal. I don't wanna be a criminal. I'm a qualified refrigeration expert; all I need is a criminal record, ruin me career before it starts.

Paul That's the deal.

Louis Okay then. Here goes. (*He gets on the floor.*) Hope there's no snakes.

Jan   No snakes.

Louis   This heat, this heat they start hatching right poisonous snakes. Just be my luck, poisonous snake bite me balls off.

He wiggles.

Paul   Okay then . . . before he's got going . . . those old geezers it's all over in two minutes.

Louis   How do you know he's old?

Paul   If he can afford a Rover 3,500, he fucking must be.

Jan   Go on then.

Louis   I'll just slide down there and nick his keys then.

Paul   Have a look in the ignition first . . . make sure he ain't left them in the ignition.

Louis (*leaps up*)   Wish you'd make up your mind! Okay then. (*Down again.*)

Pause.

And you'll be right behind me?

Paul   Yeah.

Louis   If he gets nasty – you'll be right behind me.

Jan   We will.

Louis   Okay, ta ta.

Louis *slides off.*

Jan   He's on his way.

Paul   He's athletic, in't he.

Jan *sits on floor smoking.* **Paul** *addresses the audience.*

Paul   Cousin, he says – it's all a con. All a con, know what I mean? He's a great con-man. Started on the milk round first of all, like. Learned a lot. Didn't bother with housewives and that. Robbing his own class. Shops like, he'd make about sixty quid a week. On the fiddles. First week, he'd go short himself . . . say charge twenty crates instead of twenty-one. Next week, charge for twenty-two. If they spotted it, he'd say, Last week I did meself short. And he could prove it. If they don't say nothing, proves they ain't checking, so he sticks at twenty-two. Never get too greedy . . . just a tenner a week. Each shop. I was in the boozer with him one night and this geezer comes up to him, manager of a little supermarket. Geezer says to my cousin: 'You cunt. You was doing me a tenner a week for years.' Cousin right embarrassed – see by then he'd moved on from the milk round . . . Geezer said . . . 'I didn't mind you doing it, you kept it in decent proportions. But this new bloke, he got too greedy, so I told him to piss off. His fiddles was getting in the way of me own racket.'

Jan   Louis is taking his time.

Paul   Better get them keys . . .

Jan   Yeah . . .

Paul   Me cousin bought a Jag. Gear he wears now. House he's gonna buy. Near a park, for the golf like. Only way.

Jan   You'll work for him?

Paul   Later . . . get a licence, be a driver for him. Screaming along the motorways. Cross-Channel ferry in the middle of the night. Drop off the motor in Paris or where have you and home for tea. Oh yeah, when I get me licence.

Pause.

When I get me licence.

Enter **Louis** *jangling keys.*

Louis   I got 'em!

Paul   You got 'em son?

Louis   Course I got 'em, course I got 'em, I said I was gonna get 'em, I got 'em. Didn't I. Here.

Tosses keys at **Paul** *who catches them, rejoicing.*

Paul   He got 'em.

Louis   I got 'em.

Jan   Great.

Louis   Great – I was fantastic. Easy. Like greased lightning, way me fingers went. His arse going up and down, up and down. Terrible it was, pong. He kept farting.

Paul   What?

Louis   And belching and farting. Fart, belch, fart, belch. Blimey – the bint, she must've bin deaf and . . . what d'yer call it if you can't smell?

Paul   Dunno.

Louis   That and all. I was great – where was you? You says you was gonna be right behind me, right behind me you said in case he got nasty, in case he saw me.

Paul   I knew you'd do it, knew I could rely on you.

Louis   Having a fag – me getting farted at by this great hairy arse.

Jan   Have a fag.

Louis   I'll have one me mum nicked from her place. Oh shit. (*He takes out cigarette packet. It's crumpled.*) Look.

Jan   Have one of these.

Louis   Ta. I could make a fortune picking pockets.

Paul   Easy, in't it?

Louis   Dead easy. If you wanted to do it, I mean. But only if you wanted to do it. I ain't gonna start thieving. Down the slippery slope, that is – no stopping.

Jan   What?

Louis   That's what the careers teacher said at the training course. When I was training to be an expert. Good on you son, he says. Get trained up, then there's no risk of being on the dole and sliding down the slippery slope.

Paul   All that.

Louis   That's what pisses me off.

Jan   What?

Louis   Being all trained up and still on the fucking dole.

Paul   Phone me cousin.

Paul *goes and* **Jan** *hands* **Louis** *a match.*

Jan   Have a light.

Louis   Yeah, that's nice. Need a fag after that. She was right young.

Jan   Yeah?

Louis   Right pretty.

Jan   Was she? Me Uncle Harold says there's nothing like a flash motor for pulling young bints.

Louis   I think she was a bit pissed off with the belching farter.

Jan   Well, you would be, wouldn't you.

Louis   Beautiful motor . . . what a motor . . . Oh, I'd arf like a motor like that.

Jan   Louis.

Louis   What?

Jan   If you hadn't done your training course –

Louis   I wouldn't be a refrigeration expert, would I.

Jan   If you hadn't done it, and the dole, for the whole year – and at the dole they said about – like, taking this job, in the factory . . . with the bints, like . . .

Louis   Yeah?

Jan   Would you?

Louis   Oh, well . . . gotta stand by your entitlements.

Jan   After a year though . . .

Louis   Well . . . why?

Jan   See.

Pause.

Louis   What?

Jan   I took it, didn't I.

Pause.

Louis   What, the job in the factory with the bints?

Jan   I said, I said – yeah.

Louis   You must be mad, boy.

Jan   It was seeing the bleeding careers officer on the dole, weren't it. Threw me, didn't it. I dunno . . . and never having no money – just temporary like, only till something proper comes up like.

Sudden smashing of glass.

Paul *appears kicking glass and staggers towards them holding a telephone on a lead which he has ripped out of the kiosk.*

Paul   Cunt.

Jan   What?

Paul   Cousin, phoned him . . . said . . . got the motor . . . said . . . got this lovely sparking, shiny new Rover 3,500 – and, added bonus, I said – we nicked the keys I said.

Louis I hope you told him it was me who nicked the keys.

Paul And he says . . . says, says he don't want a fucking brand new Rover, wants one of the old ones, the old posh ones, like what the olduns drove – he wanted a fucking old one.

Jan Oh, fuck it.

Paul Fucking liberty . . . fucking laughed at me didn't he. I thought he'd –

Pause.

Thought he'd be really impressed . . . nicking the keys, thought he'd . . . thought that'd right impress him, nicking the keys.

Louis Your eye's bleeding.

Paul When I kicked in the phone kiosk . . . (*He tosses away the receiver.*) Think a bit of glass went in me eyeball . . . can you see it?

Jan Nar . . . Christ . . .

Louis Won't see it here . . . under the light.

Paul Aw fuck it, maybe it's a gnat or something . . . stinging.

Jan It's bleeding . . . must be glass.

Paul Gnats bleed, don't they.

Louis Oh yeah, if you hurt it – a gnat'd bleed. Everything bleeds, if you hurt it.

Paul Fucking stinging . . . fucking cousin . . . fucking car.

Louis I was just saying to Jan here, I was saying – that bloke, talk about fart. He farted and belched the whole time he was –

Paul Yeah, well – he can go and fart and belch his way home . . . give us them keys again . . .

Louis   In me pocket, why –

Paul (*takes keys*)   Chuck the fucking keys in the fucking duck pond. Let him walk home, fat-arsed prick.

He throws the keys off. Splash.

Jan   Yeah, serves the bastard right.

Louis   I nicked them.

Paul   Yeah, well – that motor's no good to me cousin.

Louis   I might have got attacked when I was –

Paul (*screams*)   Wrong motor. (*Quiet.*) Wrong motor, weren't it . . . (*Pause.*) All he did was . . .

Jan   What?

Paul   He laughed.

Silence.

Hope he has a bloody long walk.

Louis   Yeah, serve him right.

Jan   Yeah.

Louis   I'm going home then.

Jan   Waste of fucking time. Again.

Louis   Oh. (*Rummaging in pockets, inspects keys.*)

Paul   Let's go home.

Louis   Hang on, hang on. Oh no, I don't believe it.

Jan   What?

Louis   Fucking keys you chucked in the duck pond . . . wrong fucking keys. They was my keys.

Jan   How do you mean?

Louis   These are the car keys.

Jan *and* **Paul** *fall about laughing.*

Louis   Ain't funny!

Paul   So what? Your mum's in anyway, kick the winder in and get in. Bleeding eye . . . right stinging, you sure there ain't . . .

Jan   Get in the light.

Louis   Nar, that don't matter but they was me mum's keys . . . her work key's on the ring . . . for the security . . . they was her keys you've chucked in the duck pond.

Paul   Wait a minute, you telling me . . . all night you've been walking round – and in your pocket, the fucking keys to where your mum works, where they're having the banquet, where she knocks off all great legs of ham and fags and fuck knows what – that what you saying?

Louis   Chucked her keys away, yeah.

Paul   Shit . . . we could have been up there, knocking off some of the booze and . . . could have gone up West, spotted a motor and . . . you cunt.

Louis   Don't call me that. You gotta be careful who you call that. Bloke might turn out to be fucking Kung-Fu champion or something.

Paul   You ain't.

Louis   No, course I ain't . . . but I'm just warning you in case you said it to someone who was.

Paul   Get them fucking keys . . . get them and up to where your mum works and knock off something . . . won't seem like a waste of time then.

Jan   Yeah.

Louis   Gotta get them back for the morning . . . for her.

Paul   Come on . . . Feels like a fucking needle in me eye . . .

Darken stage. Sound of splashing about in water. In the darkness we see the three lads with trousers pulled up to their knees and holding matches, lit to see with.

Louis   This is ridiculous.

Jan   Shut up and keep looking.

Louis   What if there's lizards or crabs in here?

Paul   They didn't go to the middle . . . keys only round the edge here . . . I was right pissed off they never got to the middle.

Jan   Something . . . nar, just a bit of metal.

Louis   This is really stupid . . . really stupid.

Paul   You're the stupid bastard . . . telling us all about the knocked-off legs of ham . . . knocked-off fags . . . walking round with the fucking keys in your pocket . . . what else does she bring home?

Louis   Some booze . . . she brought some champagne home . . . saving that for Sylvie's wedding.

Paul   She getting married?

Louis   Will one day.

Paul   Who'd marry her?

Louis   You'd be surprised.

Paul   Surprise me.

Louis   Hello . . . bloody bat! Jesus, bloody bat –

Paul   Ain't a bat you prick. Pair of knickers caught up in the trees.

Louis   Thought it was a bat.

Jan   Is it a bird, is it a plane – no it's –

All   Batman.

They hum the Batman *theme. Then after two times,* **Louis** *sings.*

Louis
    Batman,
    Hanging on a lastic band
    Fell into a pot of jam
    Along came Spiderman
    Thought he was a bogey man and
    Eat him!

They laugh.

Sing that to me brother's baby. Right likes me singing that.

Jan   Be able to sing it to your baby brother.

Paul   Yeah . . .

Jan   Shh . . .

Pause.

Louis   What?

Jan   So quiet . . . never heard it so quiet . . .

They listen.

Paul   Here . . . down here . . . thought it was here somewhere, by this sign . . .

He holds up the keys, with the other hand he holds his eye.

Jan   Fantastic!

Paul   Here, catch Louis –

He throws a stone. **Louis** *dives and a great splash.*

Louis   You stupid arsehole!

Paul   Nar . . . that was a stone . . .

Paul *jangles the keys.*

Louis   I'm soaking in mud, ain't I.

Jan   Be a fast runner . . .

Paul Dry off . . . come on . . . get up there in that geezer's motor . . .

Jan Hey, get dressed . . . get a move on . . .

Jan *and* **Paul** *splash off.* **Louis** *strikes a dramatic pose.*

Louis All mud and slime . . . smothered in mud and slime . . . like Jimmy . . . there's this scene . . . in *Giant* . . . when no one don't wanna know . . . see . . . don't wanna know and he's on his own and no one wants to know, takes the piss outa him and then he finds oil don't he, on this bit of land, like . . . and they're all sitting there, all these people who take the piss out of him 'cause they think he's a right wank . . . and there they are, sitting in their posh clothes on the . . . outside the house . . . and they see him coming . . . and he's all smothered in oil . . . he looks right black, looks like a black . . . all oil all over his face and hands and clothes . . . and he stands there arms up, like a gladiator or something . . . and he just looks at them, he just looks . . . whites of his eyes staring . . . 'cause he fucking knows . . . fucking knows what they think of him . . . but now, different now . . . he's fucking got 'em. I liked that bit. Liked that bit.

He does his James Dean look at the audience. Sound of a car starting off. **Louis** *hesitates, then runs off. Blackout.*

Sound of end of 'God Save the Queen'. A triangle of light floods out from an open door off.

Voice And now, my lords, ladies and gentlemen . . . the loyal toast. Be upstanding and raise your glasses. Her Majesty the Queen.

Voices Her Majesty the Queen.

Applause.

Voice And now, to address this banquet . . . our most distinguished guest . . . Our Youth Employment Officer, Mr R. Kershaw . . .

Applause.

Out of the doorway comes **Jan** *with a crate of wine. Then* **Paul** *with his arms full of champagne, brandy and whisky bottles. Then* **Louis** *with a ham and a huge chicken. They hold fingers to lips. All this very silent. They set the stuff down stage centre.* **Jan** *and* **Louis** *return to the room.* **Paul** *opens a champagne bottle. Fizz and bubbles. He gulps it down.*

During this . . .

Voice   My lords, ladies and gentlemen . . . A time for rejoicing, a time for celebration. But this year, the usual end of term pleasure in our schools will have been overshadowed by the tragic statistics of youth unemployment – something that rightly and properly is being described as the most worrying social problem of the seventies. The fact of the matter is, there are now 253,379 school-leavers on unemployment registers in the United Kingdom and as the school year did not end in some parts of the country until after this month's count was taken, the figures in August will be still worse. But the problem of youth unemployment is not confined to those who left school this summer; there are now more than 100,000 youngsters who have now been unemployed for more than a year and this month's figures will include many more who are destined to accompany them along this depressing and potentially destructive path to adulthood . . .

By now **Jan** *and* **Paul** *have come out with more bottles. They all have one open and sip from champagne and switch drinks, getting drunk very fast.*

Paul   Shut the fucking door then . . .

Louis *shuts the door and we only hear a murmur of speech.*

Jan   So much gear –

Paul   Just getting chucked away.

Louis   So much, they'd never notice some is gone . . .

Paul Jesus, this bleeding eye.

Jan (*looking*) Can't see nothing . . . oughta get up the hospital with that . . . in case it is a bit of glass . . .

Paul Stopped bleeding, anyway.

Jan Put all this in the motor and drive it home . . . flog it. Easy eh?

Louis I dunno about that . . . dunno about that . . . that's criminal.

Paul Right!

Louis I don't wanna blemish me career.

Paul What fucking career? You ain't got one.

Louis I'm trained.

Paul Trained for what? They just got you outta the way for a year you prick.

Louis But I'm trained though . . . ain't I.

Paul This is lubberly . . . lubberly bubbly.

Jan It rhymes.

Paul Rhymes . . . I foresee a great future for meself . . . get this in the motor . . .

Jan Same motor . . . say the cops is looking for it though . . .

Paul Fuck the cops . . . yeah, maybe . . . another motor . . .

Louis Hey, hey hey hey . . . look . . . it's an old one . . .

Jan Bloody Rover 3,500 – old one.

Louis Ain't left-hand drive but . . .

Paul That's the one, that's the one . . . how handy . . . how convenient. That's exactly the one me cousin wants . . . and a little Union Jack on the bonnet . . . how pretty.

Jan I'm starving . . .

Louis Chicken here . . .

Jan Bit of that . . .

Paul Bit of that scotch . . . nick that motor . . . drive it up the fucking wall . . . that's what I'd like to do.

Jan Get pissed, throw up over them snobs in there . . .

Paul Open up the motor . . . bung the stuff in there . . . Oh great.

Louis Looks so nice and shiny . . . black and –

Paul Yeah well – soon have all that paint off . . . new numbers . . . new engine number and . . .

Louis Looks very polished and looked after . . . pity it's gonna –

Paul What?

Louis Well, get – you know.

Paul Sod that . . . get the stuff and . . .

They get the stuff, then turn and pause.

Jan Shit.

Paul Getting in it.

Louis Posh sods.

Paul Bloody bloke with a bloody lavatory chain round his neck.

Louis Daft geezer with him . . .

Jan Bloke from the fucking job centre, in't he . . . bloke who said I'm choosy . . .

Louis They're going . . . car's going . . .

Sound of the car moving away. They make V-signs.

Jan   What we gonna do with all this then?

Paul   Chuck it back in through the winder?

Louis   I could refrigerate this. If I had the tools and equipment.

Paul   Yeah, all that.

Pause.

Louis   Take what we can carry then?

Paul   Yeah, take what we can carry.

Jan   And . . . not take the other motor?

Pause.

Paul   I'm too pissed to drive. Might drive it off the bleedin' road and we'll all get killed. Like Jimmy!

Louis   Yeah. If he hadn't got killed, he'd be nearly fifty now.

Jan   Fat.

Paul   Bald.

Louis   Nar, he'd still be a rebel!

Jan   Take what we can carry then?

Paul   On the tube.

Louis   Yeah, better than getting killed.

Jan   Right.

Jan *and* **Paul** *exit with bottles, hams etc.*

Louis   Yeah, us getting killed. What a fucking waste that'd be.

Louis *exits with his arms full of champagne bottles.*

Fast blackout, music loud.

Abide With Me

A play in three scenes

Abide With Me was first presented by the Soho Theatre Company at the Soho Poly Theatre Club, London, on 28 September 1976, with the following cast:

Paul	Karl Johnson
Jan	Philip Davis
Louis	Elvis Payne

Directed by Keith Washington
Designed by Vivienne Cartwright

Scene One

The sound of a soccer crowd roaring and singing. Lights up on an empty stage: a corrugated iron wall, rubbish on the floor.

Jan *runs onto the stage in full tribal costume – Doc Martens boots, army trousers rolled to the knees, thin braces, no vest, waistcoat, and scarves tied round his head and dangling from his wrists and waist, like a pirate. He leaps up and down – trying to look over the wall.*

Pause.

He paces, then – enter **Paul**.

Paul Well?

Jan No . . . no joy yet.

Paul No joy, what do you mean no joy? Nothing?

Jan No.

Paul Is that what you're saying? Are you saying you blew it? Are you saying: 'I fucked it. It's all a blow-out'? Tell me Jan, son – what are you trying to say? I mean – what are you saying?

Jan No joy.

Paul Oh Christ, oh fuck it.

Jan I did me best.

Paul Best, ha. What about your Uncle Harold?

Jan Ah well –

Paul Ah well my arse.

Jan I reckon me Uncle Harold. I reckon our chances with me Uncle Harold.

Paul I reckon your Uncle Harold is all sat down nice and comfy with a bottle of scotch and his chicken legs by now.

Jan Nar.

Paul   And that only if your Uncle Harold managed to stagger past all the hundred odd pubs on the way without collapsing into a drunken stupor on the pavement.

Jan   If he could find a bloody pub open. Bastards, closing all the pubs.

Paul   You and your Uncle Harold between you have – you pair have really fucked it.

Jan   You ain't done so hot.

Paul   I put a lot of faith in you, Jan, son. I believed in you. I had – faith in you. 'Jan won't let us down.' I've been telling everyone that all week. 'You won't get into Wembley without tickets,' they kept telling me. I said, 'Maybe no chance if I weren't going with Jan. But Jan and his Uncle Harold – irresistible combination,' I said. 'I wouldn't be surprised if I don't end up sitting next to Callaghan and Mark Phillips and tonsil teeth herself,' I said.

Jan   I did me best.

Paul   Yeah. Your best.

Jan   This is a good spot here. We can see right down Wembley Way. If we keep looking, we're bound to see me Uncle Harold.

Paul   Only a hundred thousand people pouring down Wembley Way, son. And a few extra thousand like us who ain't got tickets. How we gonna catch sight of your Uncle Harold from here, then?

Jan   His hat. I saw his hat. We'll spot his hat from here. I saw it on Thursday night. About a four-foot top-hat, red and white stripes with a couple of red and white balloons on top.

Paul   Fantastic.

Jan   If you see a bloke strutting down Wembley Way who looks about ten feet tall, that's me Uncle Harold.

That's our tickets, Paul.

Paul   He's got three-quarters of an hour. He'd better
have them.

Jan   He won't let us down.

Paul   I've heard that before.

Jan   He won't.

Paul   We'll see.

Jan   He's great for tickets. Fantastic.

Paul   So far, that has not been confirmed by my personal
experience.

Jan   For the semi-final he had two tickets for the
directors' tea-room. I saw 'em. He showed me them. He
said, 'Jan son, I'd very much like to give you one of these
tea-room tickets.'

Paul   Yeah?

Jan   He said, 'Jan, I'd really like to give you one and
come in for a cuppa with me and Matt Busby. And all of
them. The high and mighty of Old Trafford. But –
unfortunately it's spoken for.'

Paul *grins savagely.*

Jan   He said, 'I've already promised this tea-room ticket
to the bloke who flogged me the cost-price carpets I fitted
in Lou Macari's bungalow. Otherwise, it'd be yours.' I was
right choked.

Paul   I'd have choked your Uncle Harold.

Jan   But, see, it's all long-term planning. By taking the
cost-price carpet bloke in for a cuppa with –

Paul   The high and mighty of Old Trafford –

Jan   'That way,' says me Uncle Harold, 'I'm assured of
similar favourable cut-price carpet transactions thus

enabling me to acquire additional tea-room tickets for future matches which I shall then pass on to you, he said.

Paul   I don't want a ticket for a cup of tea! I want a ticket for the fucking Final. The climax of the season . . . this memorable, monstrous season. To see U-ni-ted smash to pulp those country bumpkins of poxy Southampton. Christ, there'll be more goals behind that wall this afternoon than – even the bloody *Mirror* says you'll need an electronic calculator to keep up with the score. On the telly last night they said it'd be the first final to reach double figures since they wore braces and shorts down to their ankles. I gotta see it, I gotta see it. I gotta see it.

Jan   We will, don't worry. Me Uncle Harold won't let me down. Or me mates.

Paul   He'd better not.

Jan   He's got enough and more besides.

Paul   How's that?

Jan   The players – the players' perks.

Paul   Liar.

Jan   Listen, in the last couple of weeks he's fitted a carpet for Alec Stepney's bedroom and let Gordon Hill have a twenty-five-foot length for his sun lounge less than cost price. 'I lost money,' he said. 'I lost money on the deal – for you and your mates.' He said. Great carpets and all. So that they can walk about the house with no shoes on . . . to gently manipulate their feet. They showered him with tickets, out of gratitude.

Paul   I believe it all. When I've got the ticket in me hand, when I'm inside.

Jan   Maybe Louis –

Paul   He's taken his bloody time. We said meet here.

Jan   Fancy working on Cup Final morning.

Paul   On *the* Cup Final morning. Teams'll be coming out in half an hour . . . Oh Christ. I gotta be there . . . fucking hell, ain't missed a match all season . . . Eight quid on train fares every other Saturday . . . eight quid on fares just to see the home matches . . . every bloody match I've seen and when it comes to *the* match, the bloody Final . . . oh Jesus. Gotta see them, Doc's Red Army . . . marching out . . . gladiators . . . lush emerald turf . . . band playing . . . sun beating down . . . shining on the Doc's bald spot . . .

Jan   Me Uncle Harold said he's had a hair transplant.

Paul   I suppose your Uncle Harold fitted it cost price. Behind here . . . fifty yards away . . . the bloody goalposts. (*He beats his fist on the wall.*) Behind this wall . . . if it weren't for this wall . . . Smash it down . . .

Jan   Don't worry, we'll get in. I feel it. The main thing is . . . we're here . . . on the day.

Paul   Yeah.

Jan   Drink in that atmosphere . . . I wish Cup Finals was at night . . . the atmosphere at night matches . . . sixth round at Molineux . . . that Wednesday night . . . fucking felt it . . . throbbing . . . and I thought they'd had it.

Paul   Two down – nothing . . . always come back, never give up . . . like ants . . . they can cross mountains . . . stamp on them, crush them, and they just keep coming, teeming at you . . . I knew we'd win . . . I felt it . . . in me blood . . . bubbling . . .

Jan   I'll never forget that night . . .

Paul   Weren't a bad night in Sheffield . . . after the Derby match . . .

Jan   Jesus. Don't know how I come to be holding that copper's hat . . .

Paul   If they'd seen it!

Jan   Chucked it out the window.

Paul   All that and . . .

Jan   It'll be all right, I tell you. And we're here. Wembley on the day. Better than watching it on the telly. It wouldn't be the same.

Paul   That's true. It wouldn't be the same. Mind you, it wouldn't be a bit fucking bad . . . actually seeing the match.

Jan   Uncle Harold won't let me down.

Paul   Matter of fact, I've got my doubts about your Uncle Harold. I started wondering about him when he painted his house red and white stripes.

Jan   He said it's the only house in Ardwick red and white stripes.

Paul   I believe that.

Jan   See it from the end of the street.

Paul   Hardly . . . unnoticeable.

Jan   Neighbours went mad.

Paul   Think it was bleeding ice-cream parlour.

Jan   It were just after he painted it me Auntie Elsie left him.

Paul   Ha.

Jan   She said, 'You care more about Manchester United than me.'

Paul   Ha.

Jan   He said, 'I care more about fucking Stockport County than you.'

Paul   If Louis uses his loaf . . . on his way up . . . the touts and that.

Jan   Didn't see none.

Paul   There must be touts. What's-his-name, Flash Sid
or something – get tickets for anything, he says. There was
this article in the paper about him. Frank Sinatra, Royal
Box at Ascot . . . When there was that farting about,
Princess Margaret, you know, and the Queen says to her,
'You'd better piss off for a bit, ducks.' And Margaret says,
'Nar, I wanna see Wimbledon. The final like.' So the
Queen says, 'No chance, I ain't having you in the Royal
Box with me, scandal you've caused.' But come the
Wimbledon men's final, there was Margaret – sitting in the
front row of the Royal Box. Queen right annoyed. She
says, 'How'd you get here?' Margaret says, 'Flash Sid
touted a ticket for me.'

Jan   Really?

Paul   Fuck off.

Enter **Louis**, *breathless. Also in tribal clothes.*

Jan   You took your time.

Louis   Trouble I've had.

Paul   Aggro?

Louis   No, not that. Bloody mum – hid me bloody Doc
Martens didn't she.

Jan   What? (*He laughs at* **Louis***'s fancy shoes.*)

Louis   Hid me Doc Martens. When I got back this
morning, to get changed – she'd been through me
bedroom. She thought there was going to be a lot of aggro
today, and – scatty cow – she hid me boots.

Jan   Bit bloody strong.

Louis   An' she'd gone out. Out the way. These are
killing me. Bought them for Sylvie's wedding – only worn
'em once. Well, we got them?

Paul   Bit of . . . a hold-up.

Jan   Haven't seen me Uncle Harold yet.

Paul   Much happening tout-wise?

Louis   I only saw one and –

Pause.

I feel right stupid without me Doc Martens. I'll kill her when I get home. If she's chucked them away –

Paul   This tout?

Louis   He only had one.

Jan   You got it!

Paul   To be on the safe side, Louis, mate.

Louis   He didn't have three. He only had one.

Paul   You got it?

Louis   No . . . no I never got it.

Jan   As an insurance, we said if we got offered one – get it, we can always flog it when Uncle Harold –

Paul   Louis, son – why didn't you get it? How much did he want? A hundred quid? A grand? A bleedin' Concorde in part exchange?

Louis   Well, see –

Paul   Did you see it?

Jan   Hold it in your hand?

Paul   Feel it between your fingers?

Louis   There was only one – there's three of us.

Jan   We could have tossed for it.

Louis   But –

Jan   Gone Hickory Dickory Dock for it.

Paul   I could have practised me Kung-Fu on you for it.

Louis   It weren't like that.

Paul   I'm surprised touts have the neck to try it for the
Red Devils – the Stretford End mob, mate – they'll turn
his skin inside out and his feet'll end up where his ear-'oles
are.

Louis   What I'm saying though – he weren't such a bad
bloke.

Paul   A tout?

Jan   Me Uncle Harold said they're leeches. Vampires.
Sucking all the goodness out of the game for a fast buck.

Paul   He should know all about that.

Louis   What I'm saying is, he weren't such a bad bloke.
Not like a proper tout. See, he had two tickets. One for
himself and one for his son. Only last night, his son had to
go into hospital. Appendicitis. So this bloke said, he only
wanted cost price for his son's ticket. Him being a United
fan. He said he didn't want to blaspheme his ideals and the
sense of occasion.

Paul   He what?

Louis   And I had it in me hand and . . .

Pause.

Jan   What, Lou?

Louis   There was this other kid . . . with his uncle . . .
and this kid had come from Australia. To see the Final.
And so this bloke, who was flogging his son's ticket, he was
just about to flog it to me and he sees this kid crying. Cos
he didn't have a ticket. And so he says to him, 'Where do
you come from son?' And he says, 'Johannesburg.'

Jan   That ain't Australia.

Paul   Bloody South Africa, ain't it.

Louis   He says, 'Johannesburg.' And his uncle says, 'All
them thousand of miles. He's a great United fan,' the uncle

says. 'I send him the *Manchester Evening News* and the programme every week. And he comes specially, and he can't get a ticket.' So the fellah says, 'I'll give you me son's ticket. For nothing.' And this kid, he can't believe his luck. He just starts howling again. With happiness. And the fellah says to me, 'You don't mind me giving it to him, do you? 'Cause he come from further than you.' So he took it. And went.

Pause.

Paul *and* **Jan** *look at each other.*

Jan   His mum nicking his Doc Martens has affected his fucking head.

Paul   Great son, great. Fantastic. Very decent of you. Highly appropriate that.

Louis   The kid had never seen United play –

Paul   We spent about five hundred quid this season, travelling the bloody country watching them, getting them here – and you give away a bloody ticket to a geezer that ain't never seen them play!

Louis   I was a bit confused. All the excitement and bustle down there. And I've never met an Australian from Johannesburg before.

Paul   No wonder they wouldn't let you join the Army.

Louis   Hey-a, they would have done. I almost did. They wanted me. The recruiting officer would have had me like a shot if it was up to him.

Paul   And you hadn't failed your intelligence test.

Louis   That weren't the reason.

Jan   Shit.

Louis   I didn't fail it, anyway. I just . . . didn't get a satisfactory mark. That's all. There's a helluva difference between failing and not getting a satisfactory mark.

Paul After what you've just told me, I tell you – I'll sleep a lot happier from now on knowing you never got in the Army mate. Just see you, face to face with the Russian invading army – you ask them where they've come from, they say, 'Moscow', and you say, 'Help yourself kiddo, seeing you've come from so far.'

Louis That weren't funny. It all happened so fast, I was confused. One minute I had it in me hand and the next . . . I cocked it up.

Jan Don't worry Louis, I'm sure me Uncle Harold won't let me down.

Louis Anyway, I can't talk Russian.

Jan They all talk English. Everyone talks English.

Louis You should hear me old man. He don't.

Paul No mocking the Reds. This situation, us here, stranded like – this come-about wouldn't come about in Russia.

Jan Wouldn't it?

Paul Tickets for everyone there. Everyone. Say like, if Moscow Dynamo gets to the Cup Final, right. What they do, the commies, the commies go round everyone's house in Moscow and they say to them: 'Do you want a ticket for the Final?' If they can prove they're a regular Dynamo supporter, that is. They say, 'Yeah', and the commies get them all to stick up their hands, all of those that want to go to the Final and then, say if Dynamo's playing . . . some other mob or other, well, they goes to where this other team hangs out and they say to everyone there –

Jan Providing they can prove they're a regular supporter –

Paul Of course. Goes without saying. They say, 'Stick up your mits if you wanna see the Final,' so they all sticks up their mits and they get counted and then they all get tickets. Very fair that. Only the true fans get in. None of this dishing out tickets left right and centre to Princess Anne and her bloody handmaids and horses and what have you and women who don't know a football from a blown-up Durex.

Louis   What happens if more commies want to see the Final than can get in?

Pause.

Paul   They build a new stadium.

Jan   Christ, that's rich.

Louis   And still they're pouring in . . . look at them . . . I never seen so many people. They can't all get in. When all the Stretford mob who ain't got tickets turn up . . . oh Christ, Paul – they'll storm the gates, smash 'em down, pour in, hundreds and thousands of us. We can all sit round the greyhound track.

Paul   You ever stormed a gate, mate?

Louis   Nar, but –

Paul   But, but, but, but. I tried that at Upton Park when they locked us out. Oh yeah. Very happy experience that was. 'Storm the gates,' some bastard at the back hollers. They stormed the gates all right. I was the bastard at the front. Me nose buried in the gate like a bleeding woodpecker. They want to storm the gates let them . . . follow them in, at the back. That's what I'll do. I ain't no battering-ram.

Jan   Don't worry, it won't come to that. Uncle Harold won't let me down. Did you see anyone in his hat?

Louis   Ah, well – there was this bloke by the station with a big red and white top-hat . . . so I asked him if he was Uncle Harold only I couldn't remember his name then, so I said: 'Is your house red and white stripes?' He said, 'No but me budgies are.' Turns out he was Southampton. Cunt.

Paul   That's Southampton for you. Bloody yokels, bloody all cowhands and shepherds and that. It's very odd a team that don't come from a big city. Dirt and grime and factory chimneys. It's unnatural.

Jan   I hate Ipswich. All that bloody fresh air. No wonder no one can play there.

Paul   Ipswich ain't bad. I mean, compared to Southampton, Ipswich's like bloody Birmingham.

Louis   I hate Birmingham.

Jan   Wouldn't mind Francis though.

Paul   He wouldn't fit in. Not the new style. Not the go go go. Mind you, if we changed styles, if we wanted Francis, he'd come like a shot. He'd take a drop in wages to play for United.

Louis   Who wouldn't?

Paul   These cunts at Southampton. Bloody Channon and –

Louis   He's good.

Paul   He ain't bad, be okay if he played for a city team. But he's got a farm or something. Slows him down. Everything's so slow then, see. You do everything so slow when you're on a farm, it gets into your system. Unless Channon joins a big city club, he's finished.

Jan   Look what happened to Osgood.

Paul   Proves me point. Now Osgood weren't arf bad at Chelsea. Bit of a fairy, but, not bad. Goes to Southampton – last time I saw him, every time someone pushed a ball through for him to chase, he stood thumbing a lift. He won't get a kick all afternoon.

Louis   See 'em coming up Wembley Way. Load of wankers. No loyalty. Like on a day out. Don't mean nothing to them.

Paul   Yeah well, don't let that deceive you. Nasty
bastards living around the Dell. Year we come up, bloody
herded through from the station to the ground we were . . .
like bloody sheep . . . cops shoving everyone. Step into the
road to get out of the crush and the cops hammered you.
Oh, it felt great. They was fucking shitting themselves. I
felt – fantastic.

Jan   Was there any –

Paul   No . . . no bother at all . . . just the look of us
stopped that . . . like Denis Law, you know . . . just his
look, how it used to be . . . way he stood there, with the net
bulging, hands up . . . chin out . . . fucking worship me,
slaves, get on your fucking knees . . . and all the defenders
scattered about, hating the cocky bastard, yet nothing they
could do . . . 'cause it was just the way he looked.

Louis   I wish I'd seen Law.

Jan   You ain't seen nothing if you ain't seen Law.

Louis   I wish I started coming with you a season earlier,
then I'd have seen him.

Jan   I don't know how he could have joined City . . . I
don't understand that . . . Christ Almighty, I even went to
bloody Southampton once, to cheer on bloody
Southampton 'cause they was playing City. Five quid that
trip . . . without the beer money . . . screaming for wankers
like Paine and bloody gongly Davis . . . hoping they'd tank
City . . . Bloody City won three–none.

Louis   I wish I'd seen Law . . .

Paul   Oh, you never saw nothing if you never saw Law.
So cool. I happened to be in the dining-car with old Lawy
once . . . coming back from Burnley I think it was . . .

Jan   I'm glad they're down, I hated that trip.

Paul   Twenty quid . . . Anyway, I was in this dining-car,
like . . . and the waiter was right nervous, 'cause he was

serving the King . . . shaking the waiter was, this one
dishing out the peas. 'Peas, sir?' he asked Lawy. 'Just a
few,' said Lawy, Scottish voice, you know. Like Rod
Stewart tries to put on. Then the train goes through this
tunnel and rattles about, come out the dark and the
waiter's dropped the whole great bowl of peas on Lawy's
lap. Now Paddy Crerard or Besty would have lipped him,
right? Not Lawy. He just turns round and goes: 'Waiter, I
said just a few peas.'

They laugh.

Jan   Bit different from coming back from Millwall . . .

Paul   Oh Christ, I'll say. Couple of years ago this was,
Lou . . .

Jan   Coming up from Division Two.

Paul   Week before, Millwall mob had really gone on the
rampage . . .

Jan   At Bristol.

Paul   Everyone in New Cross shitting themselves . . . we
were nice and quiet . . .

Jan   'We're the best behaved supporters in the country.'
Sang it all the way from the station.

Paul   Cops frog-marching us . . . keeping us apart . . .
then they started chucking stuff – rocks, cans of blue
emulsion paint . . . blue hair I had for a month . . . bright
blue. I had to wear a bloody hat all the time.

Jan   They started saying . . . chanting, they started their
chant . . . all hell broke loose . . . they started chanting . . .
'Munich 58', 'Munich 58', 'Munich 58'.

Paul   Shits. All them that died . . . I bleeding cried all
night . . . and then I'd never heard of Duncan Edwards . . .
remember me old lady came into me bedroom. Me and
Pam was just waking up . . . me mum howling and she
don't give a fart about football . . . she was holding the

Daily Mirror and eyes all red and she said . . . 'They're dead. Busby's babes. They're dead.'

Silence.

Just saying it now . . . feel the shivers going through me . . . bloody dead . . . broken bones and . . . Pam started crying, just a kid . . . in the same bed as me . . . I held her as she cried . . . and I swore, I did . . . when I left school, an' had the money I'd do anything, go anywhere, die, if necessary, for that club . . . for Manchester United.

Pause.

Jan   Understand Lou?

Louis   Yeah . . .

Jan   And Matt, Matt in hospital – saw the newsreel on telly when he retired . . . sitting up in his hospital bed, eyes full of tears, saying, 'We start again.'

Pause.

He's a great bloke.

Paul   The greatest.

Jan   Bit old now but –

Paul   Bit old, but – great bloke.

Jan   Me Uncle Harold said, when he was in the tea-room with him –

Paul   What?

Jan   He said, 'Matt Busby is a great bloke.' He said, 'He's a saint.'

Paul   That is a compliment, coming from your Uncle Harold. He'd know all about saints.

Jan   I know he won't let me down.

Paul   Half an hour . . . kick off.

Jan   Give him another five minutes and then . . . if – he was delayed or . . . have a look see what prices they're touting for.

Paul   Right.

Louis   Listen to that . . .

The crowd is singing:

> *'Que sera, sera,*
> *Whatever will be, will be.*
> *We're going to Wem-ber-ley.*
> *Que sera, sera.'*

Louis   Makes me feel –

Pause.

I like that. You know, this year Paul –

Pause.

Paul   What?

Louis   I sure glad I'm with you . . . places I seen this year. I ain't done nothing before this year. Best thing that ever happened was going to the factory, meeting you.

Paul   Oh.

Louis   I'd have just stayed a Millwall supporter, same as everyone else around home, if I ain't met you.

Paul   You could never have stayed a Millwall supporter Louis. Spiritually, you're the Red Devils.

Louis   Oh Christ, yeah. But –

Pause.

Hard to feel it, you know. Without me proper gear. Wish me mum hadn't hidden them. See, she thought there was going to be a lot of aggro.

Paul   It's the Cup Final for Christ's sake. Anyway, that's all paper talk. Bloody papers.

Jan   Papers full of it for that Cardiff match. That's what started it. 'Streets of fear,' they said. And all these Welshmen barricading their windows and closing pubs and setting dogs on us. Then they blame us for protecting ourselves. Papers make us sound like animals.

Pause.

Louis   That singing . . . like church.

Jan   Church?

Louis   I . . . me mum and dad used to make us all go to church. Didn't you never go to church?

Jan *and* **Paul** *look at each other.*

Louis   Singing makes me think of church, choir and that.

Paul   You've found a new religion now.

Louis   Right. Got to have faith in something.

Paul   The Reds!

Louis   I just wished . . . weren't so far to go every other week.

Jan   If they had any gumption they'd move to London. If Manchester United played all their home matches in London, capital city – they'd have 200,000 a week turn out. On average. Everyone'd flock to them. Arsenal'd get no one.

Paul   Leave off you daft prick. The whole point of Manchester United being in Manchester is – you stupid prat.

Jan   I just meant.

Louis   It'd save a packet if they were.

Paul   No better thing to spend money on.

Louis   No. No, no better thing.

Pause. They listen to the singing.

Jan   At least we're here, on the day.

Paul   Oh, we're here. And we're going to see the match.

Jan   Uncle Harold won't let me down.

Louis   Such a beautiful day for it.

Jan   All weathers, the team that wins the cup.

Louis   What?

Jan   The team that wins the cup – all weathers.

Paul   What's he going on about?

Jan   I mean, the team that wins the cup – they've got to be able to play in all weathers.

Paul   Oh yeah, definitely.

Silence.

Jan   All weathers, the team that wins the cup.

Paul   Definitely. Hey –

Jan   What?

Paul   Look . . . coming up there –

Jan   Christ, the top-hat . . . looks like him . . . well, can't see him, but looks like his top-hat. See I told you, he wouldn't let me down . . . that's me Uncle Harold for you.

Paul   You sure it's him . . .

Jan   Wait till he gets past that row of coaches . . . see, I'm like a son to him, his favoured son, he says. After me dad pissed off, me Uncle Harold come round one night, he was really great to me . . . had this bike he give me . . . said to me mum, 'I shall treat Jan like me own favoured son.' I told you he wouldn't let me down, that's him, that's him all right. I won't be a tick . . . this is it boys –

Louis   Fantastic!

Paul   Bloody great.

Jan   We're in . . . won't be a tick . . .

Paul   Get a move on then . . . wanna see the teams coming out.

Jan   Right. (*He dashes off.*)

Louis   Relief.

Paul   Nar, see Louis son, I told you you'd be all right with me. I told you.

Louis   Yeah. This morning, you know –

Paul   You shouldn't have gone in this morning, you know Louis.

Louis   The overtime –

Paul   Oh sure, the overtime. But not Cup Final morning.

Louis   When I said I'd do it, I didn't think that it was Cup Final morning. They all thought I wouldn't get in –

Paul   Jealousy.

Louis   Eh?

Paul   They're jealous. Bloody jealous. See Louis, before I went there, they hadn't had a real Manchester United fan at the Self-Opening Tin Box factory.

Louis   Yeah?

Paul   I was unique. They talked about me . . . I could hear them. Above the noise of the machines, I was on the tin-cutting machine then. The din! But I could hear them . . . see 'em pointing me out . . . 'cause I was unique.

Louis   I'm unique and all now.

Paul   No one else in the spray shop been where you've been this year, seen what you've seen. How many in the spray shop have been to . . . Carlisle, Peterborough, Newcastle and Manchester twenty-four times this year?

Pause.

Louis   None. They all get me to talk about it . . . to talk about it you know. Specially old Lil. I miss her.

Paul   She weren't such a bad lady. Size of her.

Louis   Must have been all of sixteen stone. Hey, did she –

Paul   What?

Louis   Don't matter.

Paul   Go on, what?

Louis   I'm not saying nothing against her like.

Paul   Don't matter if you are. She's left.

Louis   That was great. She always used to say, 'If I win the big prize on the bingo, the golden four thousand, you know what I'd do? I tell you what I'd do: I'll go right up to Reginald Baker and say: "You know what, Regional Baker? You're a big cunt but it ain't as sweet as mine."' (*He laughs.*) And when she won the golden four thousand, she did!

Paul   Yeah, and I remember what Mr Baker did afterwards. No knocking off five minutes before . . . for a wash and brush up . . . bastard sped up the conveyor belt . . . so at first you didn't notice. There was thirteen thousand cans coming through an hour . . . gallon paint cans and all . . . I'm surprised he ain't got the Queen's Award for Industry yet.

Louis   Paul. Did she grope you?

Paul   Eh?

Louis   Ol' Lil . . . did she finger you?

Paul   How do you mean? Exactly?

Louis   When everyone went to the canal bank dinnertime . . . and she switched off the lights in the spray

shop . . . did she used to put her hand down your trousers
. . . an' feel you?

Pause.

Paul   Is that what she did to you?

Louis   I thought she did it to everyone.

Paul   Jan and his Uncle Harold are taking their bloody
time.

Louis   I can't see them.

Paul   How often did she do that?

Louis   What?

Paul   Old Lil.

Louis   I don't wanna talk about it . . . she was disgusting.

Paul   I didn't know about that.

Louis   The other boys told me – she did it to everyone
who worked in the paint shop. Christ, it was hot in there
this morning – under the glass roof, heat of the drying
ovens . . .

Paul   Did the other women know?

Louis   Eh?

Paul   The other bints in the spray shop – Hair Lacquer,
and Flossie, and that red-haired one with the rubber
gloves.

Louis   Well, that was the point.

Paul   What was the point?

Louis   At first, in the dark see . . . see, it was really hot,
last summer when I started in there . . . and I sat down on
the rags in the corner, for a kip, you know. And I must
have dropped off . . . and when I woke up, there was old
Lil next to me. She was breathing like an old chimney, you

know . . . with her big hands down me pants . . . she was really sweating . . . trying to push her tits in me face and that . . . Christ, I laughed.

Paul Laughed?

Louis She was laughing and all. And then I saw the other bints . . . they was laughing . . .

Pause.

I'm glad she's left.

Paul Right. Come on Jan, for Christ's sake, get a move on.

Louis She weren't a bad lady.

Paul I wonder why she never done it to me?

Louis She only does it to the young kids.

Pause.

Paul That's what the factory does for you . . . makes everyone look old and washed out.

Louis *laughs.*

Paul I tell you something Lou boy, they wouldn't fucking try it nowadays . . . see us coming with our Red Devil gear . . . right . . . like the factory . . . no one tries nothing . . . see it, don't you . . . in their eyes – fear.

Louis Envy.

Paul Terror.

Louis I was no one till . . . someone now.

Paul You don't need the bloody Army, Louis – you're in the best bloody army there is . . . ten minutes, in there – whole legions of us . . . Doc's Red Army . . . our drills and Doc Martens and bob hats . . . union jacks and tartan and no shirts, whatever the weather . . . Christ they envy that . . . singing . . . chanting . . . fever starting and they'll be out . . . jogging, dead nonchalant . . . out into the arena out of the dark and into the sun . . . like bleeding gladiators . . .

The crowd noises off swell, increase in volume.

Doc in front . . . in his best suit . . . rolling the Wrigley's in his mouth . . . Martin Buchan behind . . . on his toes, knees bobbling . . .

Louis   Buchan and Forsythy – they're all Scottish, Christ I wish I was Scottish . . .

Paul   Brian Greenhoff, he ain't Scottish – Hilly, bleeding Cockney –

Louis   Christ, Hilly – fucking ace. Pearson . . . dynamite both feet . . . and Stepney. Cockney an' all.

Paul   Houston – Coppell . . . Dally . . . McCreery . . . McIlroy and . . .

Louis   Lou himself.

Paul   Gotta be there, gotta be there –

Great roars.

Enter **Jan** *in tears.*

Paul   Jan –

Louis   Hey, what's up?

Jan   I . . . I . . .

Paul   That was yer Uncle Harold –

Jan   Yeah –

Paul   Well, you got them?

Jan *hesitates.*

Jan   See, the bloke with him was the bloke who –

Paul   Didn't he have the tickets then?

Jan   He had them but, what I'm saying is: the bloke with

him was the bloke who let him have the carpets cost price.
And he's asked the bloke who services his carpet
showroom vans cost price.

Paul   Shit.

Jan   And the garage bloke brought his son.

Paul   Fuck.

Jan   And the bloke down his road who put in a bathroom
suite cost price.

Paul   Oh . . . Oh great.

Jan   Me Uncle Harold was really sick about it.

Paul   Yeah?

Jan   He said, Jan – I feel as if I've let you down.

Paul and **Louis** *exchange looks.*

Paul   Very sensitive bloke your Uncle Harold.

Jan   Oh, he is. He knew how sick I felt. See, he'd done
his bit, he'd got a ticket for himself and another three.

Paul   Hat-trick.

Jan   He said the carpet bloke had talked him into it. In
the Albion last night. He said if the carpet bloke hadn't
bought him six double scotches . . . he said he knew he was
being conned. So he went to the bog for a piss, to think
how to get out of it, and he pissed over the garage bloke's
Hush Puppies. So he give him a ticket as a way of
apologising.

Paul   If he'd thrown up, I suppose he'd have given him a
handful?

Louis   But how could he do it, Jan? I mean – how? He'd
promised them to us –

Jan   He said, he'd use his best endeavours.

Louis   What?

Jan   I mean, be fair – that's . . . Oh Christ.

Pause. **Jan** *really cries.*

Let you down . . . I let you down . . . sorry.

Pause.

Louis   Weren't your fault, Jan.

Jan   He promised me.

Paul   If I see him.

Pause.

He better not let me see him. I'll fucking . . . Jesus, I'll
open his face with a fucking bottle. Take out his eyes with
a corkscrew. Ground a bottle in his face till it's freckled
with splinters of broken glass. He'll be a fucking Red Devil
all right. All blood! (*He stands breathing heavily.*) Behind that
wall – (*He shrieks.*) Behind that wall. If it weren't for that
wall. (*He runs at the wall; smashes himself into it.*)

Jan   Sorry Paul.

Silence. **Paul** *looks for something to smash.*

Paul   Still time, find a tout . . . get a ticket, there must be
hundreds. All them celebrities that get the free ones, they
unload them on the touts. No problem, we'll have tickets
all right. We'll be in there. Might miss the teams coming
out. But we'll be in there, all right. No trouble.

Pause.

Leave it to me. I'll shoot down there . . . Lou, you look for
a tranny – bloke on the hot-dog stall over there had a
tranny – get the tranny, while he ain't looking. Nick his
tranny.

Louis   Could have watched it on telly at home – not
stand here listening to it on a tranny –

Paul   Take the tranny inside. Watching the match and

then we listen to the interviews with the players afterwards.
Right?

Jan   Yeah . . .

Paul   You Jan, son. You can get some hot dogs to nosh.
Some cokes and all. Distract the bloke while Lou fingers
the tranny, right?

Jan   Right!

Paul   Gonna be all right, in't it.

Jan   They was only standing seats.

Louis   Tickets – standing tickets.

Jan   Uncle Harold was choked about that. He said he'd
expected seats. He said we'd be better off with seats
anyway.

Paul   I'll get seats then.

Jan   Right.

Paul   Your bread –

Jan   Go up to . . . twenty quid.

Louis   Twenty?

Paul   You got twenty?

Louis   Well . . . okay.

Paul   What better thing to spend money on anyway?

A crescendo of roars off. The band starts to play 'Abide With Me'.

Jan   Oh Jesus . . . they've brought it back.

Paul   'Abide With Me'.

Jan   They stopped it at the Cup Final. I thought they
stopped it at the Cup Final.

Paul   They brought it back . . . for United. Wembley
anthem.

Louis   It's a hymn.

Paul   If the band hadn't played this hymn, Doc's Red Army would have fucking killed 'em.

Jan   Makes me go cold.

Louis   They . . . sung this at church a lot . . . when I used to go. I didn't know it was part of the Cup Final. Didn't know then. Always liked it. I asked the preacher once, I said, 'What's it mean?'

Paul   Mean?

Louis   'Abide with me,' he says. 'It means – like, tolerate. Means tolerate me. Like if you do a lot of things wrong, there must be a reason, so He . . . tolerates you.

Paul   Stuff all that. It means Wembley, the Cup Final. United in that tunnel, banging their studs on the cement . . . smelling of liniment and shirts brand new, smelling brand new . . . and waiting, ready to go out into the sun. We'll be there, get these tickets and –

He hesitates.

The singing of 'Abide With Me' is very loud. **Jan***, then* **Louis***, and finally* **Paul** *join in the singing, standing holding their arms up, scarves stretched between their hands. They sway in time to the music. The hymn swells.*

The lights dim to fade. The music continues louder.

Scene Two

The same, later.

Roaring crowd behind the wall. **Jan** *sits on a rubbish bin, listening to a transistor radio.* **Louis** *paces, eating a hot dog, sipping a coke.*

Jan   We're all over them. We're murdering them. It's going to be a rout. Hang on – (*He listens to the radio.*) Fucking hell, that was Hilly! Turner blocked it with his feet. Bloody feet. Oh yeah, we're murdering them. Great, fantastic.

Louis (*no enthusiasm*)   Yeah.

Pause.

Paul's taking his time.

Jan   Yeah, didn't think . . . didn't think it'd take this long.

Louis   Jan . . .

Pause.

Jan   What?

Louis   We're going to get in, aren't we.

Pause.

Jan   Paul'll sort it out. Paul's magic, for sorting out stuff. We never had tickets for Hillsborough. Paul sorted it out.

Louis   Different at Hillsborough. There was more tickets. Clubs get a better allocation for the semi-final. It's bloody lousy, way it is for the Final. Why don't they give enough for all the true fans.

Jan   Well, see, like me Uncle Harold explained it. It's an occasion. A national asset the Cup Final. That's why it's not just the finalists' fans who get in. That's why they give a third of the tickets to dignitaries. He said.

Louis   Dignitaries?

Jan   Well, see. Like . . . celebrities, who make society tick.

Louis   Eh?

Jan   I dunno, I didn't understand it.

Louis   Sixty thousand week in week out at United. What about the Irish fans?

Jan   Christ, yeah.

Louis   Every week from Dublin, they said. Twenty-seven quid it costs them, to every home match. Great blokes. Great blokes.

Jan   Yeah, I really like it when we're on the same train as them.

Louis   None of them had tickets for the Final.

Jan   No, well – they're Irish.

Louis   They spend twenty-seven quid for every home match. They don't earn much. All their money for United, and then they don't get to see the Final.

Jan   Well, the dignitaries –

Louis   What fucking dignitaries?

Silence.

Jan   Well like – this is how me Uncle Harold explained it. Like see, the Arabs. They wanted to see the Cup Final.

Louis   I want to see the Cup Final.

Jan   Well like, now they've got all this dough. Like, if they want to buy a fleet of warships or something, to smooth 'em up, so they buy British ones, like – what happens is, the Ministry of Defence gets onto the FA, like and says, 'Give us twenty tickets.'

Louis   Yeah.

Jan   Then they buy the warships.

Louis   Right.

Pause.

All them women though – they ain't buying warships.

Jan   Wives and that. Bints who knock about with dignitaries.

Louis   Bint on TV last night – she didn't even know both teams had the same colours.

Jan   No, she didn't.

Pause.

Pearson's having a brilliant game according to this –

Louis   'Ark at them. Oh Christ. How high do you reckon that wall is.

Jan   I dunno.

Louis   Maybe we could get over it.

Jan   Glass at the top.

Louis   Yeah, but . . . what's a bit of glass – to see United in the Final?

Pause.

Yeah well. There's hardly anyone down there now.

They look.

Jan   Me grandad hated football.

Louis   What?

Jan   Just thinking. Ol' Grandpa, he hated football he did. Said he stopped watching it after the war. Said, 'All them years of war fighting the Germans, then we play them at football.' 'Football's better than war,' I says. 'Yeah,' he says. 'They should have thought of that before they started the war.'

Louis   It'd been fairer if there was a queue, you know, you could queue for tickets.

Jan   Yeah.

Louis   Starting, say, right after the semis. You queue up. First come, first served.

Jan   I'd have queued for days.

Louis   Weeks.

Jan   I'd have taken me holidays to queue.

Louis   Right.

The crowd roars.

What was that?

Jan   Turner just got in the way of Daly – let fly. What a boy! We're all over them, the country bumpkins don't know what day it is. Eh, what's that? Bloke here reckons McCalliog's playing . . . not bad.

Louis   McCalliog. He can't play.

Jan   Course he can't play. Stands to reason, that Doc wouldn't have let him go if he could play. The Doc saw him, thought – Christ, what a wanker, you can go. He can't play.

Louis   No.

Jan   Bloke here don't know what he's talking about. Says he's playing all right. Shows bloke here don't know nothing.

Louis   If I was the Bionic Man –

Jan   If I was the Bionic Man, I could see through that bloody wall.

Louis   That's what I mean.

Jan   Or leap over it.

Louis   Right.

Pause. **Louis** *mimes the Bionic Man.*

Jan   Tell me, Bionic Man – what can you see?

Louis   Oh, it is great, son. It is fantastic. I wish you could see what I can see. The colours . . . the movement. Darting about . . . in their blood-red shirts – shorts so white . . . Southampton in gold and blue . . . pitch as green as a rubber plant and the crowd swaying with their flags . . . The ball's orange . . . looks like a billiard table. It's great.

Jan   All I can see is a wall . . .

Louis   You ain't the Bionic Man . . . Just see James Dean standing outside Wembley – if he wanted to get in.

Jan   Eh?

Louis   Old Jimmy, he'd just crash through the wall, he would. Nick a motor, and smash through the gates.

Another roar.

Louis   What was that?

Jan   Oh, that was Southampton – miles wide and over.

Louis   Stepney had it covered.

Jan   Yeah.

Louis   Did he say that?

Jan   Goes without saying.

Louis   Osgood can't shoot, not from thirty yards and no one'll let him get closer than that.

Jan   It weren't Osgood. It was McCalliog.

Louis   No danger.

Jan   No.

Louis   I mean, if McCalliog was the sort of bloke who ever looked like scoring, the Doc wouldn't have let him go.

Jan   Right.

Pause.

Louis   If I had a length of rope and an anchor, we'd be in.

Pause.

A length of plastic-coated, grade three rope and a metal hook with a claw, we'd be in.

Jan   How?

Louis   Commando training. Commando training mate. Oh, a wall like that. Show a wall like that to a commando and he'd piss himself.

Jan   Yeah?

Louis   Even a green recruit with just three weeks' basic training, show him a wall like that and he'd piss himself, he'd say: 'You must be joking mate.' With just three weeks' basic training, plus the equipment – the plastic-coated, grade three rope and half a dozen anchors – you'd get five hundred commandos over that wall and inside in three minutes.

Pause.

Jan   Pity we ain't got no rope or anchors.

Louis   Yeah.

Jan   Is that what you tried to sign up for?

Louis   What?

Jan   A commando?

Louis   Oh, not a commando, no. I wouldn't mind being a commando, but I didn't try that. I mean, they only take the cream, just the cream. I thought: well, I know I ain't the cream. You've got to be the cream. I didn't think it was worth trying the commandos, since I didn't have a chance. I thought I'd try something where I had a chance, you know. Avoid the frustration of getting turned down.

Jan   Yeah.

Louis   So I tried what I thought I had a chance, a good chance. That's what bugged me, getting turned down.

Jan   It would.

The crowd roars.

Hilly, header – over.

Louis   We're murdering them.

Jan   Yeah. There was a mate of mine who went to Paris. And he got really pissed, so pissed. On that aniseed drink. Makes you really pissed, so next morning, if you drink a glass of water you get pissed all over again.

Louis   Commandos ain't allowed to touch that stuff. Not allowed to drink, except after a mission successfully accomplished.

Jan   Well, he was in the Navy, see.

Louis   Rum.

Jan   And he ended up in Paris with a few blokes and got smashed out of his head on this aniseed drink. An' he signed up for the Foreign Legion. Walked in pissed and said, 'I want to sign up. So they give him the form and he signed up. For thirty years. And when he sobered up he was in the Sahara.

Louis   Christ.

Jan   Only another twenty-seven years and he's out.

Louis   Jesus.

Jan   His mum was arf annoyed.

Louis   I wish me mum ain't hidden me Doc Martens.

Jan   His mum said to my mum, she said, 'Tony he's always been difficult, always had problems with him. But this time he's gone too far.'

Louis   I wouldn't mind joining the Foreign Legion. To forget.

Jan   Yeah.

Louis   If I wanted to forget, I'd sign up like a shot.

Jan   He'll be an old man when he comes out.

Louis   There's some vicious bastards in the Foreign Legion. Vicious.

Jan   He don't send nothing home neither. At least when he was in the Navy he sent something home.

Louis   They've been playing fifteen minutes.

Jan   Yeah.

Louis   Paul'll go spare if we don't get in.

Jan   It ain't my fault.

Louis   I'm not saying it's your fault. Put it this way: I wouldn't like to be in your Uncle Harold's shoes if Paul sees him.

Jan   No.

Louis   He shouldn't have done that, Jan. Shouldn't have promised.

Jan   How do you think I feel.

Silence. The crowd is gently murmuring off.

Enter **Paul***. He looks livid. He paces, turns, grimaces, smashes his fist against the wall.*

Jan   No luck?

Paul *glares at him.*

Paul   Fucking tout – asking, asking twenty-five quid for a standing ticket. Twenty-five quid for one. Jesus.

Pause.

Louis   Bit steep.

Paul   Held it up, he did. In his hand, held it up. Said, 'How much am I offered?' Great crowd round him. Blokes in suits, ties and that. Posh voice, said 'Thirty quid.' He got it. Cunt. Flash cunt. (*He paces about again.*)

Jan   We . . . ain't gonna get in, are we?

Pause.

Louis   I was saying, if only I had a thirty-foot length of
rope and an anchor – over the top.

Paul   Is that all you need? What have I got here? (*He pats
his pockets.*) Electric toothbrush, complete works of Charles
Dickens, packet of three, six light bulbs and a set of
sparking plugs but . . . no anchor and no thirty-foot length
of rope. Sorry.

Pause.

This is disgusting. Disgusting. This shouldn't be allowed.
Shouldn't be allowed. Twenty-odd times I've been to
Manchester this year. An' to Wolverhampton, Burnley,
Sheffield. To Birmingham, Ipswich, Villa Park,
Newcastle, Liverpool, Middlesbrough, Derby. An'
Leicester and Stoke and Leeds and Coventry. All that, on
fares. Standing in the train, five hours . . . eight hours . . .
standing up in wet clothes, no fucking food on the train
. . . standing up in the rain on the terraces . . . like . . .
cattle. No roof to keep the rain off . . . Lavatories stinking
like cess-pits. Warm beer in paper cups . . . no food at the
grounds . . . herded about by the cops. No wonder they
call us animals. That's how they fucking treat us. (*He
growls, impersonating an ape.*)

Jan *and* **Louis** *laugh, goad him on. He behaves more ape-like. He
stops.*

Paul   They treat dogs better. That's 'cause we're fucking
animals, Lou, son.

Louis (*acts ape*)   Yeah.

Paul   Treat people like animals, that's how they act.
Those bloody lavatories at most of the football grounds in
England if they were like that at the factory Lou,
everyone'd walk out. Strike until they're cleaned up.
Bloody clubs expect you to pay to get into them.

Louis   I reckon I missed about fifteen goals this season,
'cause I couldn't see.

Paul   Whole day and twenty quid to see the match at
Coventry and I couldn't see either fucking goal. Talked to
this bloke who went to Holland one year . . . see United
against Ajax. Oh, it's a different world over there. Never
have to bother over there . . . sit down . . . bring round
beer and lovely hot food, waiters do . . . while you're sitting
there, while the match is on . . . like a fucking night club,
not like a football ground . . . all the geezers take their bints
. . . great.

Louis   Like cricket.

Paul   Eh?

Louis   Never have no riots at cricket.

Paul   Well, not often.

Jan   Never have no aggro at Wimbledon – tennis and
that.

Louis   Treat you better. You can see. Get something for
your money more than the game.

Jan   Don't exploit you.

Paul   You what?

Jan   Me Uncle . . . Tom –

Paul   Oh.

Jan   Said he hates being exploited. His governor
exploited him he said. He told him what to do. Where to
go.

Paul   I wish . . .

Pause.

There was something else. To make me blood bubble, to
look forward to . . . to . . . mean something.

Pause.

There was this boy I used to know . . . a student, at the

factory, one summer . . . for a bit of pocket money, he
worked a couple of weeks . . . then Mr Baker found out
about him and got him out of the factory so fast you
couldn't see him move. Junkie, see. Oh yeah. I saw him
after, in the High Street. Said it happened at the Black
Lion. Lot of pushers there. An' he didn't want to know.
They pumped him with the stuff. Held him down and shot
it into him . . . and then, later, after he'd got hooked, they
wouldn't always sell him it, 'cause they kept putting up the
price. See. An' he said, 'Cunts, they got me hooked an'
then said no.' (*He paces, turns.*) Bloody football clubs. Get
you hooked, get you boiling, get the fever rushing through
you – all of them, build it up, get a head of steam and then
when it explodes, wash their hands of you, call you
animals, say piss off we don't want you. (*Pause.*) An' they
know they've got you hooked. That you can't do without
them. That seems more of a crime to me. Than the crimes
we're supposed to do.

Louis   At least we'll be able to see it on the telly
tomorrer.

Paul   Fucking Jesus.

Louis   That's blasphemy.

Paul   So what. God's dead. They killed him in the war.

Louis   No.

Paul   Up there, laid out his corpse and wrapped it in a
sky-blue shroud. Shows he was always a fucking
Manchester City supporter.

More roars off.

Christ, what's happening. Jan, what's –

Louis   A goal! We've scored! We're winning –

Paul   Nar, weren't loud enough for a goal. Jan, the
radio.

Jan (*struggling with it*)   Bloody dial – busted.

Paul   What – give's.

Jan   Bloody dial fucked, or the batteries gone flat.

Louis   What happened? Gotta know what happened –

Jan   I can't help it –

Paul   Pissing hell.

Louis   It must be a goal, it must be a goal!

Jan   Sod it.

Louis   We're winning – we must be winning –

Paul   Get that radio –

Jan   I can't Paul, it's smashed.

Paul   Smashed, I'll fucking smash it – (*He hurls the radio against the wall. The plastic casing smashes, the radio falls to the floor in pieces.* **Paul** *stands breathing raggedly.*)

Jan   You've busted it . . . we'll never find out who scored now.

Louis   I wanted to see that . . . wanted to see that.

Paul *lets out an animal cry and runs against the wall, smashing himself against it.*

Louis   Paul, for Christ's sake.

Paul   If it weren't for that wall.

Louis   Paul, don't be a stoopid bastard, you'll –

Paul   There's always a fucking wall in the way. Always get so far, and there's a wall to block it. Smash it down, smash it down –

He charges it again. **Louis** *tries to stop him.* **Paul** *hits the wall and screams. He crumples to the floor. A great roar from the crowd.* **Jan** *and* **Louis** *approach the wall.* **Paul** *lies there groaning.*

Jan   Better find the St John's men.

Louis   He's mad, he's crazy.

Jan   Yeah.

Louis   I wonder who scored?

The roars grow, the lights fade. Blackout.

Scene Three

Later. The sound of the crowd roaring. Lights up.

Louis *is fixing the radio with a plastic spoon. The roars continue.*

Enter **Jan**.

Jan   Still nil–nil.

Louis   Oh.

Jan   Apparently it's all United. Southampton are right knackered. They're soaking up so much punishment. The bloke on the ice-cream van said – he's got a portable telly.

Louis   See it?

Jan   Nar, there was such a crowd there. Anyway he said it looks like there'll be an avalanche in the last twenty minutes. Six or seven goals.

Louis   Great.

Jan   What you doing?

Louis   Fixing the tranny.

Jan (*looks*)   Bloody hell. You've . . . got it all back together.

Louis   Yeah, still ain't working yet, but –

Jan   I didn't know you could fix radios.

Louis   Me sister's husband, he does radios an' that. In the Navy. Wireless operator. Real skill. He'll make a bomb when he gets out. Electronics an' that. Tried to get me to have a go at it. I said, 'Leave off: I work in a factory mate. No chance.' So's he tried to show me how to do it. An' showed me how trannys work.

Jan   Christ. I didn't know you was good at that sort of thing.

Louis   No? Learned the basics on me refrigeration course.

The crowd roars.

Jan   It'll be good to hear the last fifteen minutes.

Louis   If I can get it fixed . . . see, it's the . . . I dunno how to explain it, I dunno what the things are called.

Jan   Well, so long as you can fix it – that's the important thing.

Louis   Is it?

Jan   Sure, course it is. That's what counts.

Louis   Pity the recruiting officer didn't agree.

Jan   Oh.

Louis   Told him I could fix radios. An' phones. An' alarm clocks. He said there's not much call for alarm clock repairs in Belfast.

Pause.

He was right sarcastic. The other bloke weren't so bad. He said: 'Look son, you ain't got too much going for you at the moment. But if you can prove yourself as a competent electrician, if you learn a bit more, come back in a year and we'll have another look at you.'

Jan   Oh.

Louis   At two o'clock in the afternoon.

Jan   Eh?

Louis   I wrote it down when to go back. I'll go back
then. Me brother-in-law, when he's on leave, he's going to
show me a few things. Get me to look a bit competent as
an electrician, and then, well – fingers crossed, I'm keeping
me fingers crossed.

Jan   Bit difficult mending wirelesses with crossed fingers,
in't it?

They laugh.

Louis   Come in handy on the Plain though –

Jan   Eh?

Louis   With the cadets, two weeks, Salisbury. Full
manoeuvres. Had to do everything, we did. Guard duty,
rifle range, camping, oh a lot of camping. Food never
tastes so good as when you're out in the open . . .

Jan   I remember when you come back – so energetic!

Louis   It's a different world. Just like the Army, it is. Like
a family. Looks after you, looks after you.

Pause.

Jan   More bloody reliable than me Uncle Harold.

Louis   Well –

Jan   When me dad pissed off, he said he'd treat me like
his own son.

Pause.

His son never hears from him neither.

Pause.

Me grandad always said they'd hang Harold.

Louis   They don't hang people no more.

Jan   Me grandad said they'd bring back hanging
specially for him.

Louis   You oughta join the cadets, Jan. That's what you oughta do.

Jan   I want to . . . be part of something.

Louis   Yeah –

Jan   Like when we're standing there . . . on the Stretford End . . . crushed in, thousands of us . . . and 'cause you're in the red and white, it don't matter that no one knows you, 'cause you're like brothers, so close . . . all together . . . all together . . . and all leaning together, the same way, and all breathing together, like, not thousands of people, but like one . . . like a great giant breathing.

The crowd's roars subside.

I wish it could be like that every day of the week. Better than the fucking factory.

Louis   Give it a try on Thursday . . . that way, get in, enlist, it'll be like it all the time, every day of the week.

Jan   Well?

Louis   Thursday night.

Jan   I'll have . . . a look. But I ain't saying I'll join.

Louis   Thursday then.

Jan   Right.

Enter **Paul***, his head bandaged.*

Paul   Would have to be the same fucking eye.

Jan   Paul – you all right?

Paul   Yeah, I'm all right. Couple of stitches.

Jan   Oh –

Paul   No anaesthetic.

Louis   No?

Paul   St John's bloke said, 'I'll give you a shot.' I said,

'Stuff that son, I don't want none of that. Just bung the stitches in.' Still nil–nil.

Louis Yeah.

Paul Last ten minutes, there'll be a flood of goals. Two a minute, I reckon. What you doing?

Louis Fixing the tranny. Nearly fixed it.

Silence.

Paul Didn't know you could –

Louis Yeah.

Paul Oh. You don't want to let Mr Baker hear you can fix radios. An' that. Oh, he'll have you doing all the sodding plug-fixing and that, if he knows you can twiddle with wires.

Louis I wouldn't mind that. Out of the spray shop, more money doing electrics than shoving cans through an oven.

Pause.

Paul I'd not let Mr Baker hear about that, if I was you. Right Jan?

Pause.

I said –

Jan Right.

Pause.

At least . . . we was here on the day.

Pause.

Something to tell our grandchildren.

Paul What?

Jan Here on the day . . . Man United, the Red Devils, Doc's Army won the cup . . .

Paul   Doc's Red Army, an' Doc's cockney army – we'll be marching tonight, mate . . . oh Christ . . . missed the match, but – tonight . . . marching through Piccadilly, thousands of us . . . see the lights going off in the pubs as we approach . . . be some glass flying tonight, be some glass smashed tonight . . . worse than the blitz. All together, marching through London . . .

Pause.

Just the thought of it . . . makes me wanna wet meself.

Jan   Eh?

Paul   Felt like that after the semi . . . felt it throbbing through me . . . We'll be marching tonight. Better not catch sight of your Uncle Harold.

Jan   N-no.

Paul   All together.

Jan   Yeah.

Paul   No worries, no cares, nothing to have to think about. All that obliterated, just the –

Louis   Like the cadets, Jan.

Paul   Eh?

Louis   Plunge in, no cares, all together.

Paul   Wrong army.

Louis   No.

Long pause.

Paul   You fixed that radio yet?

Louis   Almost.

Paul   Gonna be a replay . . .

Jan   Still ten minutes.

Paul   They'll close the game up now . . . too much to risk losing. Here again, Thursday night. We'll fucking have tickets then.

Louis   I thought it was Wednesday –

Paul   Thursday.

Louis   But Thursday, see Thursday –

Pause.

Paul   What?

Louis   Thursday, well, every Thursday, cadets night.

Pause.

Go on Thursdays to the cadets.

Paul   Not when United are playing.

Louis   They never play on a Thursday.

Paul   This Thursday, the replay –

Louis   But Paul . . . got to have a hundred per cent record. For the regular army, got to prove I'm hundred per cent.

Paul   Lou baby, you've gotta get your priorities right, son.

Louis   I seen all the matches.

Paul   Can't miss the replay. Can he Jan?

Silence. The crowd is roaring.

Louis   But Paul.

Paul   Can't let everyone down Lou.

Louis   Won't make no difference whether I'm there or not.

Paul (*grabs him*)   Lou, kiddo – United need you.

Louis   Need me? They don't need me. Or you. Or Jan. Don't give a fuck about us. How come we're outside if they

need us? Cadets need me, make me a part of them, take
me in, give me food, give me a home, give me . . . a job.
Give me something to do. United don't give a shit. Take
me money, that's all.

Paul   No . . . they've got us all, got you . . . you can't do
without them.

Louis   Gonna try hard Paul.

Paul   Tell him Jan.

Silence. Roars.

Jan, I said –

Jan   Gotta come Lou. Gotta come.

Louis   Want the Army, Paul. Like you want it Jan.

Paul   Jan, don't be a prick – Jan don't want –

Louis   Be someone?

Paul   Is someone. Right Jan? Down your road, when you
set out in your drills and tartan, eh?

Louis   When I set out in my cadets drills and –

Paul   Lou, son –

They struggle.

You're fucking coming.

Louis   Ain't throwing it away, boy. Ain't gonna be like
you when I'm your age. Factory six days, life on one? That
ain't a life. That ain't living.

Louis *pulls away.* **Paul** *flicks a knife, holds it towards* **Louis***.*

Louis   Aw don't be stupid. I'm on your side.

Paul   You've changed sides.

Jan   Paul . . . he's Lou.

Paul   Done things for you Lou, son, done things for you

this year. At Sheffield when they got you in the bog, twenty
of them . . . when you went in the wrong bog and they got
you, I waded in . . . kicked his fucking head in to release you.

Louis   You didn't do that for me, Paul. You did it 'cause
you get your fix kicking fucking heads in. Me, I was just
the excuse.

Paul   Did it for you . . . 'cause you're one of Doc's
soldiers.

Louis   No Paul . . . put it away Paul . . .

Jan   Not today, Paul . . . not on the Cup Final. No sense
of occasion.

Paul   You sound like your fucking Uncle Harold. Cunt –

Jan   Good bloke.

Paul   What's he ever done for you?

Jan   Visited me in the home every week, some boys had
no one visit them.

Paul   Bollocks. He was probably screwing the matron.

Jan   Paul . . . drop it, let it drop.

Paul   You're gonna be here Thursday Lou, gonna be
here at the replay.

Louis *begins to shake his head.* **Paul** *goes to lunge at him but the
crowd lets out a deafening roar. It continues loud.*

Jan   Christ.

Paul   That's a goal.

Jan   Scored!

Paul   Jesus.

Jan   Just before the death –

Euphoria. They leap about. Embrace. **Louis** *stands apart from
them. The roars continue.*

Paul   Musta been Pearson –

Jan   Hill was going close.

Paul   Radio working Lou – quick.

Louis   Working. (*He hands the radio to* **Paul**.)

Paul   Only joking see, no problem. Thursday, cadets all right. No replay now – we've done it . . . oh great. (*He holds the radio to one ear.*)

Jan   Who scored it? . . . got the station. Who –

Paul *is deathly. Pause. The roars continue.*

Paul   Stokes.

Pause.

Jan   Own goal?

Pause.

Paul   McCalliog split the defence with a long through-ball and Stokes . . . put it in the corner.

Pause.

Jan   It's not possible.

Paul   Fucking radio ain't lying.

Pause.

Oh Jesus. (*He holds his head.*)

Jan   Five minutes to go still . . .

Paul *looks at him.*

Jan   Oh Christ. (*Almost tearful.*)

Paul   How's it possible? How's it possible? After all we've done this season . . . so far, so much . . . days in trains, all that attacking, all that . . . fighting . . . pipped for the League and now . . .

Louis *edges away.*

Paul   Where you sneaking off to?

Louis   I'm going home.

Paul   Match ain't over.

Louis   It is now.

Paul   When the mob gets out . . . tonight, oh tonight there'll be fucking hell break loose.

Louis   That's why I'm going home.

Pause.

I'll come round for you Thursday, Jan.

He goes.

Paul   What's he mean by that?

Pause.

Jan   Dunno. Dunno what he means.

Pause. The roars continue.

Paul   He's gone. He's chicken. He's a wank. There, that's what happens when ol' Lil gropes you.

Jan   She used to grope everyone.

Paul   Did she grope you?

Jan   Used to, till Lou came.

Paul   I wonder why she never groped me.

Pause.

Tonight . . . oh Christ, tonight . . . it'll be like . . . He weren't trying to chat you into joining the fucking Army was he?

Pause.

Said –

Jan   The cadets, he made it sound like . . . a family.

Paul   We're your family. United, the biggest family in
the land . . . oh tonight, you'll see tonight . . . it'll be like
after the Spurs match . . . after coming back from White
Hart Lane . . . we'll assemble at Euston . . . we'll march in
file, wave after wave of us . . . the streets'll empty as we
approach . . .

The lights begin to fade. **Jan** *goes the way* **Louis** *went.*

Paul *is alone stage centre. As the lights fade, a spot continues to
illuminate his face until only his face is lit.*

Paul   They'll barricade the windows, the pubs'll lock
their doors, the lights will go off in the shops and the police
will line the pavements, white with fear . . . cops' hats'll
bobble like decorations on a windy promenade . . . the air
will be heavy with shouts and yells and the smashing of
glass . . . No one will ignore us. We will not be ignored.
They'll talk about us, write about us, hate us. Hate us.
Hate us. Animals, call us animals . . . not ignore me . . .
won't be ignored . . . not ignore me . . . not . . . ignore . . .
me.

The lights go to black. More roars.

In the City

In the City received its first production at the Greenwich Theatre, London, on 29 September 1977 as part of the trilogy entitled *Barbarians*, with the following cast:

Paul   Nick Edmett
Jan   Karl Johnson
Louis   Jeffery Kissoon

Directed by Keith Hack
Designed by Voytek

Enter **Jan** *in soldier's uniform; he speaks to the audience as though the audience were a policeman.*

Jan   What do you mean? I ain't doing nothing wrong. I'm on embarkation leave. Ain't I? Just come for the Carnival. No I ain't on duty. What, here? Leave off. This is London! Soldiers in the streets, you must be joking! I'm not telling you me name. You tell me your name copper. All right, all right . . .

Paul *enters and addresses the audience, reading a copy of* Time Out. *He wears dark glasses.*

Paul   'Attractive intelligent American woman. I'm not tired of London, but only of selfish people only wanting to receive but not to give. Wide cultural interests. Seeks attractive, aware, sensitive bachelor with crazy sense of humour . . . '

Paul *laughs crazily. He reads on silently.*

Jan   See, here's me ID. All right, going tomorrow yeah. Cross the old pond to . . . You know. Just have a good time tonight. Last few hours in London till . . . when I'm back. No, no weapons. Honest. Not when I'm on leave . . . just come for the Carnival . . .

Paul   'Sensitive gay guy, North Acton, 28, non-scener into rock films seeks active guy, 21–25, for sincere relationship.' (*He looks at the audience.*) Disgusting, filth, bloody pervert.

Jan   Thanks, very decent of you. Just, where's the Carnival? I mean, is it coming down here soon? Do you know the route?

Paul *approaches* **Jan**.

Paul   *Sieg heil!*

Jan   Fucking hot.

Paul   Will be later.

Jan   Uniform, I meant.

Paul   Oh, very nice, very smart – very you.

Jan   Feels funny.

Paul   You make me feel safe, you know.

Jan   What?

Paul   Standing next to you, I feel all safe and secure.

Jan   You taking the piss?

Paul   Nar, nar. I mean – I really am thinking, thank Christ I ain't got no Irish blood in me. No doubt about it. England rules OK.

Jan   Bloody serge though. It makes me leg itch. Especially in this heat. First couple of weeks at Aldershot, it gave me a rash.

Paul   Diddums.

Jan   It was impetigo. All sores all over me body. They got to me face. They said I looked like a werewolf.

Paul   Oi!

Jan   It weren't funny. There was a plague of it. In the barracks. Everyone had it who was going to Belfast.

Paul   Oh yerr.

Jan   Bloody sarge, he's a right hard nut. Goes for a six-mile run every day. He said it was psychosomatic. 'Cause we was going to Belfast. That's what he said. He said we was weak-gutted, goldfish-livered yellow cowards. (*Pause.*) He was a bit cross. 'Cause they had to put the posting back. MO – doctor – said we couldn't contaminate the inhabitants of Belfast. With the plague. Like, the impetigo.

Paul   Bit of a comedian, is he?

Jan   That's why they put the postings back.

Paul   How do you feel?

Jan   Oh well. (*Pause.*) You know, can't believe it's me, going. (*Pause.*) Bloody funny feeling I can tell you. Tomorrow. Embarkation. At 18.00 hours. Into the battlefield. (*Pause.*) I joined up to become a pastry chef.

Paul   Well, make mince-pies of the Micks.

Jan   Yeah, our lads'll show them. We'll fucking show them.

Paul   Give you a few memories to take tonight, son. Tonight, give you a few memories all right. Carnival, bints all lined up. Be here.

Jan   That's why I thought I'd wear me drills. You know, really impress them. Me sarge says women go weak at the knees when they see a highly trained soldier.

Paul   As opposed to a highly trained pastry chef.

Jan   Yeah.

Paul   You're a man.

Jan   I am.

Paul   A man. No doubt about it. A bit of a loon, but – a man.

Jan   A loon?

Paul   Fucking going to Belfast! You must be outa your head. I wouldn't set foot in Kilburn High Street after the pubs've closed. I thought you'd have more sense son. Got out of the posting.

Jan   I signed up for seven years. Ready to go – when Her Majesty called.

Paul   There was a hundred things you could have done to get out of it. Made out you'd gone berserk, or queer, or kept wetting the bed.

Jan   Wetting the bed?

Paul Yeah, like drink twenty pints every night and keep pissing the bed. They would have kicked you out then. Christ, course they would have. High risk you'd have been. Might have drowned the whole bloody unit. (*Pause.*) Well, enjoy tonight.

Jan Yeah. Last night in London till . . . Course I'll be back.

Paul Right. It's all arranged. Anything you want son. It's all arranged.

Jan Gonna be a great night – but this heat!

Paul Yeah well, that's in our favour. I mean, passion throbs with the thermometer. Bints, the inside of their thighs will be sticky with sweat. Lubberly. Oh yeah. They'll be going mad with passion in this heat.

Jan Will they?

Paul No doubt about it. Reminds them of their Jamaican heritage. All that. Down by the railway viaducts, poking them – they'll think they're out on the beach in Barbados.

Jan Bet none of them have been to Barbados.

Paul That's nothing to do with it. It's in their sub-conscious, 'cause they're black, see. Bung them a couple of vodka coconut milk cocktails and they're away. Beat of the old Bob Marley and they can't keep their arse still.

Jan I'll take me hat off.

Paul Good thinking.

Jan *takes off his hat.*

Paul Very punk.

Jan Well, what do we do then?

Paul Meet them here, this street corner. My one is definitely bringing one for you.

Jan Definitely?

Paul That was the deal.

Jan She send a photo?

Paul Sent a photo of herself. She didn't send one of her mate, though.

Jan She's your one?

Paul (*with a photo*) Yeah. All mine, you lucky girl.

Jan Let's have a look.

Paul Here (*He hands* **Jan** *the machine photo.*)

Jan Oh yeah, oh yeah. Looks a bit spotty but –

Paul Spotty?

Jan A bit.

Paul I thought they was freckles.

Jan Maybe they're freckles, oh yeah – they're freckles.

Paul Might be spots . . .

Jan Coloured, and all.

Paul Course she's coloured, that's the whole point.

Jan I meant the photo.

Paul Oh yeah.

Jan Which one was she?

Paul Oh yeah well, see – I'm not quite sure. I got a bit mixed up. I wrote to a lot of them, see. (*He opens* Time Out.) The ones with the biro squiggles, I wrote to all of them. But I got some of the replies and the photos mixed up, didn't I. I mean, the number who wrote back – I thought it was Christmas!

Jan Lots of letters, I never get no letters. Blokes in the barracks all get a letter now and again but . . . don't even get a letter from me Uncle Harold.

Paul   I tell you, the postman who come to me – needed a bleeding articulated lorry. I've narrowed it down. She's either (*He reads*:) 'Virgo widow from Hackney, 28, who misses male company for dancing and mutual pleasure and vegetarian meals' or she's '25, music teacher who likes yoga, Bob Marley and is slowly sinking into a morass of self-destruction'. She's warm and sensitive.

Jan   But these are in the magazine?

Paul   Yeah. That was the idea – have a crack at these. Save money, no need to put an advert in for us. Spoke to her on the blower when she sent her number and said she liked me photo and said I must be Scorpio and a bit kinky. That's the other thing. If we have a nosh later – don't.

Jan   I'm starving.

Paul   She says she can only be mutual if I'm heavily into macrobiotic grub. Her mate might be the same.

Jan   And she said meet outside a chip shop?

Pause.

Paul   On the other hand, she might be 'lively exciting bi-sexual are you similar?' (*He laughs, pockets the magazine.*) I think it must be her, since she's bringing her mate. You and me, her and her mate, tonight – once the Carnival gets going, dancing in the streets to the reggae, two spade bints, tank them up, then back to their place, four of us, getting the old sheets screwed up – here, that fucking skin rash of yours ain't contagious is it?

Jan   Nar. Wish it was.

Paul   Charming!

Jan   If it was, wouldn't be going across the pond tomorrow, would I . . .

Pause.

Paul   Cheer up, look happy for God's sake. Carnival. Bit of joy.

Jan   Yeah. Quiet though, init. I thought there'd be thousands of people.

Paul   Oh, there will be, later.

Jan   And the shops all boarded up . . .

Paul   All that bother last year, see.

Jan   Definitely meeting them here?

Paul   This road, opposite the chip shop, by the pub, chip shop, pub. Right place.

Jan   Hard getting here. They re-routed the bus.

Paul   For the procession. Oh, it's gonna be great. Limbo dancing under the motors and cha-chaing round the parking meters. All that.

Jan   What's she called then?

Paul   Rosie. Nice name, in't it.

Jan   It's a great name.

Paul   For Christ's sake Jan cheer up a bit. Bit of happiness. They're probably sussing us out. Look happy otherwise you'll scare them to death.

Jan   There's been a lot.

Paul   Eh?

Jan   Just saying, there's been a lot of deaths. Over there. The troubled province. (*Pause.*) Troubled province, carelessness.

Paul *is pacing, looking for the girls.*

Jan   Carelessness. The sarge says it's all down to carelessness. If you ain't careless, you're all right. What us lads have got to do is put a ring of steel round the city.

Ring of steel. That's what the veterans say. Ring of steel.
There's this old bloke, seen a lot of action. Oh yeah, a lot
– Aden, Cyprus. He says: 'There's nothing like a ring of
steel round the city. Like Johnny Turk. That's what
knackered him. Ring of steel round Nicosia and it was all
over.' You arf pick up a lot from these old campaigners.
Oh yeah. Should hear what they say about the Micks. Oh
dear, make you laugh. In the NAAFI. Jokes about the
Micks. Oh yeah. They ain't got a good word to say for
them. Not a real war, they say. Not all this bombs in the
High Street and snipers. Have to watch out for the
snipers. Have to watch out for the snipers. Snipers, they're
the lowest of the low. Disgusting. See, there's a lot of
snipers over there. Cross the pond. Lowest of the low.
Snipers are. See, you think I'm just standing here on the
Portobello Road, right? Waiting for our bi-sexual black
bints, right?

Paul   So many bints. (*He waves.*) Nar, can't be ours or
they'd have waved back. (*He shouts.*) Rose! (*Pause.*) She ain't
Rosie. Or Lindy.

Jan   But I'm not looking at the bints though. Oh no, no
way. That'd be careless.

Paul   Oh yeah?

Jan   See, what I'm doing is . . . I'm scouring the high
vantage points. Look at me, look at me. Right. What am I
looking at?

Pause.

Paul   The chip shop.

Jan   Wrong! I *look* like I'm looking at the chip shop but I
ain't. I'm scouring the high vantage points. The roofs.
There's a Silver Jubilee flag and a TV aerial on the chip
shop roof, right?

Paul   Right.

Jan   Don't miss a thing. I don't. Develops like an eighth sense. Up here, behind me, on the roof. 'To Let' sign in the third window along.

Paul   So what?

Jan   Did you see me turn round to look up there and see it?

Paul   Nar . . .

Jan   There you are, see. Extra sense. Scouring the high vantage points.

Paul   Brilliant, fucking brilliant.

Jan   Your life's in your eyes.

Paul   What?

Jan (*during this speech he becomes hysterical*)   Sarge says, in a little chat before our twenty-four hour embarkation leave, he says he was right proud of us, couldn't fault us lads. He said we'll all come back safe and sound because we've got our basics right. Use our eyes. Our lives in our eyes. These snipers, they're the lowest of the low. When the other fellers come back, whoosh. That's what they talk about more than the – well, they talk about the bombs and the ambushes, and . . . it's terrible these kids, look like angels, but fucking chucking bombs and . . . But it's the snipers. I've talked to a couple of the lads who've come back. They've tried to keep us apart. I mean they don't really like the lads who've come back talking to the lads who are going out there. But all this sniper talk. Oh dear. There's a couple of our lads, I mean, seriously, talk about snipers and they have to get up and leave the table. They really literally shit themselves. Watery shits. Don't even know they're doing it. Makes your stomach heave, in a knot. Just talking to you about it, I really feel that I could go to the lavatory like, could do with a good shit, just talking about the snipers. Christ, really does make your stomach do a somersault, the thought of those fucking snipers sitting up on those fucking roofs with their fucking commie guns just picking off decent fucking Brits, decent lads, just for the fucking fun of fucking shooting the fucking . . .

Jan *is crying.* **Paul** *is horrified. Doesn't know what to do.* **Jan** *heaves and pants and wipes his eyes.*

Paul   Hey, calm down son, calm down.

Jan   Bastards.

Paul   Yeah.

Jan   Bloody up there, behind the chimneys or something. Bastards.

Paul   Not here. Not here in Notting Hill for Christ's sake.

Jan   Right. But. Oh. Bit tense, you know.

Paul   That's only natural, only natural, in't it.

Jan   Yeah. Arf going to the lav a lot nowadays. Since they give us the embarkation date. Bloody lost half a stone, ain't I. Oh, well, bit tense.

Paul   You'll be all right, son. Course you will. I mean, you've really impressed me. You have. This extra sense lark. I mean I don't normally say nothing about it when I'm impressed.

Jan   Nar, you don't.

Paul   Takes a lot to impress me, I ain't exactly gushing with compliments.

Jan   Nar, I've always said that about you.

Paul   I tell you something. That thing you said, what was up there on the roof of the chip shop. I mean, that really did impress me.

Jan   Did it really?

Paul   Honest, I couldn't figure it out. How you'd

noticed. I really didn't clock how you'd seen up there.

Jan   Well, it's a knack.

Paul   You've sure got it.

Jan   Like a skill.

Paul   Very clever.

Jan   Extra sense.

Paul   You're telling me.

Jan   Been a sniper up there, he wouldn't have known I'd clocked him.

Paul   Yeah, and you would have just whipped up your gun and fucking blown the bleeder into kingdom come.

Jan   Yeah. After I'd got the okay.

Paul   Eh?

Jan   Well, see – can't just shoot a bloke 'cause he's up on the roof.

Paul   Fucking sniper?

Jan   Ah see, got to know he's a sniper.

Paul   If he's on a . . . 'high vantage point'.

Jan   But, got to get the okay. He might not be a sniper.

Paul   What's he doing on the fucking roof then?

Jan   Might be a chimney sweep.

Paul   With a shooter in his hand?

Jan   Ah, but it might be a stick to clean out a bit of the chimney that's blocked up.

Paul   Come off it.

Jan   No, it's orders. Can't shoot, till he shoots at me.

Paul   Let him shoot you?

Jan   Nar, take preventive actions, don't I. Hide in a doorway. It's all right. It's err . . . you know.

Paul   Oh yeah.

Jan   I mean, it ain't as simple as you'd think. Ireland, it's all a bit complicated.

Paul   Yeah, sure.

Jan   It's not a normal war, see.

Paul   Sure, I see that.

Jan   Have to look like you're okay. Not let on that you're . . . you know, a bit . . .

Paul   Bit tense?

Jan   Bit tense, like.

Paul   Yeah, but – it's like anything. Init. Before you go. But you know, once you're there!

Jan   Yeah.

Paul   A month's time. I bet I get a postcard from you all cheerful. You'll be wondering what you was worrying about.

Jan   Yeah, yeah.

Paul   Tonight. Last night in –

Jan   In London. Before I come back.

Paul   Before you come back. Make it a night to remember.

Jan   Yeah. I'm really glad you've fixed up these black birds. I've always wanted to fuck a spade, before I . . . you know, go.

Paul   Sure.

Jan   The old timers, they say there's nothing like spade women.

Paul   You bet. Thought we'd have made contact by now. What is the time?

Jan   20.14.

Paul   Eh?

Jan   In civilian jargon, nearly quarter past eight.

Paul (*shouts*)   Rosie, it's me. (*Pause.*) Ain't her.

Jan   Oh yeah. Funny, you'd have thought the streets'd be full of people.

Paul   Getting dark. Tonight, once it gets dark, that's when the fireworks'll start.

Louis *enters and addresses the audience. Just light on* **Louis** *who wears a silk shirt, a white suit and smokes a cigar.*

Louis   Tonight . . . after dark . . . when it really begins. They'll be coming in their hundreds, thousands, on trains and buses, on bikes, in cars, walking, running . . . for the masquerade. The sky lit up with fireworks. Dancing in the streets. Air buzzing with rum and blue beat. And laughter. Oh yeah. When times get hard, all the more reason for the masquerade. Like it goes back in history, don't it? Like, however poor you are, well – come the Carnival and you can play being a rich man. You can dress in the finest clothes there's ever been. For weeks, they've been making the costumes. The butterflies – wait till you see the butterfly men! Me mum and me sister and these other ladies, they took over this warehouse for three weeks to make the butterflies. Huge, huge. Like for the great – release! Like it's back home, here in the streets of London town. And every time anyone says, well things ain't good and things are gonna get worse, maybe one day, I go home, back to Kingston – Come the Carnival they say – no way! We make it happen here, man. Just two days, two days, that's all we need. Even the cavemen and 'at, at Stonehenge and all that, all them millions of years ago, they had their carnivals. You've gotta have your dream. The fantasy, know what I mean. In the streets, all come together. Blacks and whites and the Chinese and the

Indians, and we all . . . get drunk on the happiness in the streets. Oh yeah.

Lights to full. **Jan** *and* **Paul** *approach.*

Paul   Bloody hell – it's Louis.

Louis   Paul! Hey Jan, you did it.

Jan   Yeah, I did it.

Louis   You joined up.

Jan   The regulars. Yeah, I joined up.

Louis   You've come to the Carnival.

Jan   Last few hours. Before embarkation. I'm going to Belfast in the morning.

Paul   Bloody shaft!

Louis   Best suit.

Paul   Doing all right, eh?

Louis   Real good.

Paul   Got a job?

Louis   Yeah, refrigeration. And, got a motor. Only a van, but me own transport, like.

Jan   Better than the factory.

Louis   Army's better than the factory.

Jan   Yeah.

Louis   And where are you now, Paul?

Paul   Well, went back to the factory. For a bit. Tide meself over. Bit of a cock up. Joined Securicor, didn't I.

Louis   You was a security man.

Paul   Found I had a bit of talent for it. Started off casual like, on the marches in Lewisham, oh they was great. So, took it up full time. With Securicor instead of the Front. Bloody cosh, they give me. Sitting in the back of the old tank. This great Alsatian. I'll go back to them, when me eye clears up, you know.

Louis   Your eye?

Paul   Bit out of sorts. (*He laughs.*) Should have gone to the quack about it straight away. The glass had got in the retina, hadn't it. All the while fucking it up and I didn't know. Right shock it was when one day . . .

Pause.

Louis   I'm really sorry about that Paul, really sorry.

Paul   Good job I started off with two eh?

Louis   Well, you're really going to enjoy things tonight.

Paul   Funny seeing you like this Louis mate. All so real cool, like.

Louis   Well . . . you know . . .

Paul   Not much of the old Jimmy Dean about him now, eh Jan?

Louis   Everyone grows up.

Paul   That's true. Some of the pranks we got up to, eh?

Louis   Yeah.

Paul   That motor! Cup Final. Motor and now you've got one yourself.

Louis   Only a van, with the job, like.

Paul   Still, better than nothing.

Louis   Anyone still at the factory that I knew?

Paul   Few, few. Lot of kids there now. Don't care about nothing. Not interested in the overtime so us old hands do all right. Mr Baker died.

Louis   He died?

Paul   Had a stroke, didn't he. Just before Christmas.
Then he copped it. Best way, otherwise he'd have just been
a vegetable.

Jan   Best way.

Paul   He was the only one who could keep those bloody
young tearaways in hand. Now, they don't give a fuck
about anyone.

Jan   We was just wondering, like – the procession. Where
it comes.

Paul   Yeah, I mean. Is it this road, like?

Louis   Nar. Look, you come with me and I'll show you.

Paul   Meeting some bints, in't we.

Louis   Fantastic. Then you bring them.

Jan   They haven't got here yet.

Louis   Oh well, when they do.

Paul   Sure.

Louis   Glad everything worked out for the both of you.

Paul   Certainly worked out for you, son.

Louis   Yeah, moved here, you know. Like, all the family
here now. It's okay, like real close.

Jan   That's nice.

Louis   She's sure going to miss you while you're away.

Jan   Who?

Louis   Your girlfriend.

Jan   Oh well, she's not a regular, like.

Louis   Be nice to have a girl though, won't it. You got a
photo?

Jan   I'll ask her for a photo, if we get on like.

Louis   Get on?

Jan   Well, err. (*Pause.*) Made contact, Paul has and . . .

Paul   Pair of spade bints. Great to have a spade.

Jan   Never had a spade, I ain't.

Paul   All right, aren't they. Things they get up to.

Louis   Oh . . . (*His reaction.*)

Jan   What the blokes who've been abroad say, about nigger tarts.

Louis   Great . . .

Paul   Can't get enough, go on all night, that right?

Louis   Sure, all blacks – sex mad.

Paul   Fantastic.

Louis   You know niggers. Fuck like animals.

Paul   That's what I heard.

Louis   Because of the jungle. Like apes. And the ladies, nymphos.

Paul (*to* **Jan**)   What did I tell you son? Once they get here, oh yeah.

Louis   Oh yeah?

Paul   So I've heard, these negresses. Oh dear. Make it sound like you need to do Canadian airman's exercises to get in training for them. Bloody contortionists.

Louis   You cunt. (*He turns to go.*)

Jan   Louis, what's the matter?

Louis   You fucking pair of . . .

Jan   No offence. Just saying like, neither of us have had a nigger.

Louis   Go some place else. Fuck a dog, just the same.

Paul   Oi oi. Bit oity toity, ain't you. Integration, in't it. I'll report you to the Race Relations Board.

Louis   Disgusting – bastards. (*Again he turns to go.*)

Paul (*to* **Jan**)   What's up with him.

Jan   Dunno. Louis, what's the matter?

Louis   If you don't know, it's a waste of my time telling you.

He walks away. **Jan** *and* **Paul** *follow.*

Paul   Tell us where you and your mob'll be hanging out and as soon as these bints turn up we'll shoot round to you.

Louis   Drop dead.

Jan   Louis, it's us. Your old mates.

Louis   You talk about black girls like . . .

Jan   They don't mind.

Paul   Course they don't mind. That's what those bloody adverts are for. Bloody knocking shop.

Jan   And me last night before embarkation.

Louis   You got them in an advert?

Jan   In *Time Out*, yeah.

Louis (*incredulous, then laughs*)   Got them in an advert. Lonely hearts' club band? Lonely hearts, oh man but that's pathetic. That's the funniest thing I ever heard, you mean you – in an advert. They're for wankers, they're for the pathetic old shits. An advert for a bint, that's too too much. (*He goes, laughing.*)

Paul   Flash bastard. Who's he think he's laughing at?

Jan   He thought it was funny.

Paul   What?

Jan   Suppose it is. A bit.

Paul   Cocky spade. What's up with him? Gone a bit
bloody flash. Bit bloody holy nigger all of a sudden. What's
he think this is? It's Notting Hill, it's London in't it. Ain't
Jamaica. Taking the piss out of us. And you, you in Her
Majesty's uniform.

Jan   Yeah but . . . still, never mind eh?

Paul   I do mind. I bloody do mind. He was one of us a
year ago. Now pissed off, all niggers together. Piss off white
men. That's nice in't it, after all I've done for him. There's
two kinds of spades I hate. Spades who act like they ain't
spades and spades who're cocky 'cause they are spades.

Jan   He's become a real cocky spade.

Paul   I'll have him.

Jan   We'll go somewhere else. Cool down and . . . go up
West. Instead. I just wanna do something, you know.
Something to remember before tomorrow. Night to
remember.

Paul   I'll have him.

Jan   Shall I tell you something?

Paul   I can still hear him laughing.

Jan   I'll tell you something.

Paul   I'll fucking have him.

Jan   See, the regulars –

Paul   Eh?

Jan   In me regiment.

Paul   I told you you was fucking mad to sign up.

Jan   Didn't want the factory all me life. Anyway, all them
on the dole. Me Uncle Harold told me he'd heard they
was going to start conscription. He said: 'Join the regular

army and you'll be head and shoulders above the conscripts when they start conscription.'

Paul   Stupid prat.

Jan   Yeah, well. I wanted the catering corps, didn't I? He said so long as there's people, there's food. Get into catering and be all right. Lying sods, they said they'd have me in the catering corps. When there was a vacancy. How come I'm going to Belfast then? With a gun?

Paul   Lonely hearts' club . . . pathetic. See the way he looked at me? Coming to something, in't it. Bloody spades laughing at you. 'Cause you're white, I'll report him to the Race Relations Board – or kick his head in.

Jan   Them stewards, they look really hard, like – real hard.

Paul   That one of your skills? Knowing when someone's really hard? One kick in the right place – no one laughs at me. Climb up on the chip shop roof, drop fucking bricks on the spade's head. That's what I feel like doing.

Jan   I'm a trained killer. I know all the places to go for to kill. The nerves to strike. Bite the jugular, cigarette in the eyeball, break a back on me knee . . .

Paul   That right?

Pause.

Jan   Destroy the enemy.

Paul   Enemy ain't he!

Jan   They meant Micks. The IRA and all them.

Paul   He laughed at you!

Jan   Yeah, but I mean . . . he knew, like – the adverts.

Paul   I wouldn't be seen dead looking through them adverts for meself. I did it for you, son. Give you a night out in the city to remember.

Pause.

A black bint. Wank over the memory in the barracks.
Under the blankets when the lights are out. Winter nights
in Belfast, need something.

Jan   Don't go on about Belfast for Christ's sake.

Paul   Snipers'll be there, looking for you. (*Silence.*) He
laughed at us, cocky bastard. Spades, got it made. At
school, all mates. On the dole, all mates. Then they
disappear, you know. Wonder why that is? All mates and
suddenly . . . They disappear into their reggae clubs and
. . . never mix with us . . . the factory . . . sit at different
tables in the canteen . . . a million miles apart . . . (*Pause.*)
All that rhythm . . . all that joy . . . all their big white teeth
smiling . . . flashing in the dark . . . all their 'anything goes',
why don't misery choke them? Louis, laughing at me. He
wouldn't have been laughing if he'd seen us on the march
in Lewisham the other week, mate.

Pause.

Later, get him on his own . . . on his own . . . Just another
mugging, it'll be. They'll think, cops'll think, it was the
spades. Notting Hill. The Carnival. All the fault of the
spades. Never know it was us. Make him bleed. Shouldn't
have laughed at us. Spot him. Find him. Have him.

Pause.

Jan   But be reasonable. I mean to say –

Paul   What?

Silence.

Jan   Last night, I want . . . here . . . go up West and me
in me uniform, really pull. I'll put me hat back on. Would
have been nice, bi-sexual black bints, oh yeah, but it ain't
worked out.

Paul   Few drinks, get tanked up. You want to be part of
something. No family, not the army, and this . . . Carnival.

Won't let you be part of that. We're not part of nothing. Nothing. We're . . . nothing. Let him laugh at you?

Jan   Nar?

Paul   Let snipers laugh at you?

Jan   Nar.

Paul   No one laughs at you.

Jan   No.

Paul   You hate people laughing at you.

Jan   Yeah . . . I know I do. Know I do . . .

Paul *goes.* **Jan** *alone, just the light on him.*

Jan   They laughed at me mum . . . destroyed her. They took away her bowels, to stop it spreading. The doctors did. They gave her a plastic bag, she hated it – the bag to urinate in. She hated it, she said it was like having a bath wearing a life belt. She used to sing in the pub, by the flats. She wanted a garden. We never had one in the flats. Never lived on the ground, me mum didn't. The pub had a garden. Sit there, drinking her Dubonnet and lemonade. She used to sing at the pub at nights sometimes. They had turns and she'd get up and sing. Even when she was very ill. And one Saturday night, she had this . . . she had this lovely voice, beautiful. When she sang 'Good night Irene', old women cried. She was a legend, her voice. (*He sings:*)

Irene, good night, Irene good night.
I'll see you in my dreams.

Pause. He begins to cry.

And this Saturday night, they had this dwarf comic. He told tall stories and jokes, made me mum laugh. He said – see, there used to be a lot of blacks in there, and so he told jokes about the blacks. They liked them, I mean – well, they had to like them.

Pause.

And when he went off the stage, they never took off the
microphone. And it was still there, only about three and a
half feet from the ground. They asked for a song and me
Uncle Harold, he said to me mum: 'Give us a song, Elsie.'
And the other people, they all said: 'Give us a song Elsie.'
And she said: 'Oh no, I can't.' And then they all started
chanting: 'Elsie, give us a song.' And the man on the
piano, called Charles, he started playing the beginning of
'Good night Irene' 'cause it was like her signature tune and
eventually she got up and she was very overcome because
of all the warmth and the pub was nice, with warmth and
friendship. And she stood up and the drummer gave her
the hand microphone and still they forgot the dwarf's
microphone which was still standing right in front of my
mum. And she put up her hand to stop everyone cheering
and the piano player asked for hush and my mum said:
'I'm very overcome to know you all cared for me 'cause of
the collection from the pub to send me flowers when I had
my unfortunate operation . . . ' And she was very err . . .
moved. Moved. And in the quiet, there was this sound . . .
this noise. Coming out of the loudspeakers. Because the
dwarf's microphone was still switched on . . . it was
standing about waist height to my mother. The sound of
gushing water. The microphone picked up the sound of
my mum passing water into her plastic bag. Everyone
could hear it. Through the loudspeakers, the sound went
on and some people they . . . they . . . (Pause.) And some
people, some of the people . . . (Pause.) laughed. They
laughed.

He stops crying. Long silence.

That night at home, she got up out of bed and went to the
bathroom and drank a pint of bleach. Which killed her.
(Pause.) After that, it was very quiet at home. I went two
nights every week to the cadets and then . . . I signed up. I
don't . . . talk about it much. When I had the medical, I
didn't tell them about my mum . . . I thought it best to say
'natural causes'.

He stands there silently.

Lights from a lamppost, a scream. **Paul** *has* **Louis** *on the ground and is kicking him. There is blood on* **Louis**' *white jacket.*

Louis   Hey Paul, why why?

Paul   Black cunt.

Louis   Why the –

Jan *moves in horror towards them.*

Jan   For Christ's sake – leave him alone.

Paul   Black bastard.

Louis   Why are you doing this to me?

Paul   'Cause, I'm doing it.

Jan *tries to restrain* **Paul**.

Jan   No Paul, please. No trouble. I'm going to Belfast in the morning.

Paul   There'll be trouble there.

Jan   No trouble. I embark at 18.00 hours . . . so there mustn't be any trouble.

Paul   Kick his head in . . . get arrested, then they won't send you. Black shit. Flash nigger, you've made it boy, flash nigger.

Louis   I made a go of things, I worked hard.

Paul   Then how come it worked for you and not for me?

Louis   Because I tried things instead of just smashing them.

Paul   I tried and all.

Jan   I don't want to go to Belfast.

Paul   Don't want the factory. Securicor wouldn't have me as a driver 'cause of me eye.

Jan See Louis, they chucked him out of Securicor when they found out about his eye. Leave him Paul, you'll kill him. I only wanted a nice night out with some black bi-sexuals.

Paul Why have we stopped being together?

Louis Paul, please . . . I'm hurting.

Jan Paul, you'll kill him . . . You're pissed, you've gone berserk. (*To* **Louis**.) Sorry about this, he's a bit fed up. (*To* **Paul**.) For God's sake, all blood and snot and broken bits of teeth . . . he's bleeding. (*To* **Louis**.) I'll get an ambulance. Embarkation for me tomorrow . . . in Christ . . . just a couple of hours . . . There'll be snipers on the roofs. Up there, there's a Jubilee flag on the chip shop roof, don't it look nice? I only wanted to be a pastry chef. I thought, better than the factory and me Uncle Harold said as long as there's food there's people and you shouldn't have laughed. I'd have killed you only I've got to go to Belfast and they wouldn't let me go if I was a murderer 'cause you have to ask permission to kill.

Paul Kill him . . . kill him . . .

Louis Me dad said, no matter how bad it is, you can take it boy.

Jan I never knew me dad properly.

Paul Bleed nigger, bleed.

Louis Ah, ah . . .

Paul Keeeeeellllllll . . .

Jan I dunno why they're sending me to Belfast . . . I've got to kick you Louis so they arrest me and I don't have to go.

Police siren, blue flashing lights. **Paul** *runs off.*

Louis Run away Jan, run away, fuck off.

Jan *kicks* **Louis**. **Jan** *turns to the audience.*

Jan You'd better arrest me, I'm mad and very violent.

Louis He didn't do nothing, it was the other one.

Jan It was me.

Louis Weren't you Jan.

Jan It was me. I'll kick him again to prove it.

Jan *with reluctance kicks* **Louis**. *Pleads to audience.*

Louis He only did that so you'll arrest him and he won't go tomorrow.

Jan You'd better lock me up tonight, please. For a long time. I'll come quietly. If you promise to lock me up. Lock me up. I'm violent. I'm a trained killer. So you'd better lock me up. Please . . . please . . . (*He smiles.*) You're going to lock me up for a long time?

Louis Not him, the other one.

Jan *kicks* **Louis** *savagely.*

Louis He's only kicking me so you won't let him kill someone else.

Jan See, I did it all. I'm a trained killer. Lock me up. To protect myself . . . and society from everything you've done to me. 'Cause, 'cause . . . otherwise I'll do it back. To you. Worse.

He holds out his hands for the handcuffs.

Blackout.